THE NEW APOCALYPSE
PRACTICAL SURVIVAL GUIDE FOR THE UPCOMING DOLLAR COLLAPSE

MARK DORTMILLER

ASHIMO KITAWA

Copyright © 2025 by Mark Dortmiller

All rights reserved.

No part of this book may be reproduced in any form or by any electronic or mechanical means, including information storage and retrieval systems, without written permission from the author, except for the use of brief quotations in a book review.

CONTENTS

Introduction	vii
PART I – Understanding the Coming Storm	xi
1. WHAT HAPPENS WHEN MONEY DIES	**1**
Inflation, Hyperinflation, and Currency Collapse in Plain Language	1
Lessons from History	2
The Most Dangerous Myth: "It Can't Happen Here"	4
2. THE DOLLAR UNDER ATTACK	**5**
The Threat of De-Dollarization	5
America's Debt Spiral and the Federal Reserve's Role	6
What the End of Dollar Dominance Means for Your Daily Life	6
PART II – Protecting Your Wealth	9
3. HARD ASSETS THAT HOLD VALUE	**10**
Gold, Silver, and Precious Metals: Pros, Cons, and Practical Storage	10
Farmland, Real Estate, and Tangible Goods	11
Everyday Barter Items	13
4. DIGITAL ASSETS AND MODERN RISKS	**15**
Bitcoin and Cryptocurrencies: Opportunities vs. Vulnerabilities	15
Stablecoins and the Risk of Government Crackdowns	17
Why Electricity and Internet Blackouts Could Erase Digital Wealth Overnight	18
5. DIVERSIFYING YOUR FINANCIAL SURVIVAL	**20**
Cash on Hand: How Much and in What Denominations	20
Foreign Currencies as Backup	22
Balancing Real vs. Digital Wealth for Maximum Resilience	23
PART III – Survival Beyond Money	27
6. WHEN DOLLARS CAN'T BUY BREAD	**28**
Building a 30–90 Day Food Reserve	28
Water, Medicine, and Energy as the New Currencies	31
Learning Practical Skills That Replace Money	32
7. SECURITY AND COMMUNITY	**34**
Protecting Your Home and Property in Times of Unrest	34
Forming Local Networks for Trade and Protection	36
Why Community Resilience Beats Going Solo	37
8. THE FINANCIAL SURVIVAL CHECKLIST	**38**
Step 1: Secure Essential Assets	38
Step 2: Build Tangible Reserves	39
Step 3: Set Up Emergency Cash Flow	40
Step 4: Create a Family Go-Bag	41
PART IV – The Family Emergency Plan	43

9. PREPARING YOUR HOUSEHOLD	44
Explaining the Crisis to Your Kids Without Causing Panic	44
Assigning Roles and Responsibilities	45
Storing and Securing Critical Documents and IDs	46
10. COMMUNICATION WHEN SYSTEMS FAIL	48
How to Stay Connected Without Internet or Cell Towers	48
Setting Family Rally Points and Fallback Locations	49
Radio, Walkie-Talkies, and Analog Backups	50
11. THE FAMILY ACTION MANUAL	52
Customizable Emergency Plan Templates	52
Household Survival Kit: What Every Family Should Have	54
Practice Drills: Testing Your Family's Readiness	55
PART V – Thriving After the Collapse	57
12. REBUILDING IN THE NEW ECONOMY	58
Turning Crisis into Opportunity: Businesses That Thrive Post-Collapse	58
From Survival to Self-Reliance	60
13. BUILDING A RESILIENT MINDSET	61
Managing Fear and Uncertainty	61
Teaching Your Family Confidence and Adaptability	62
The Long View: Preparing Not Just to Survive, but to Prosper	62
CONCLUSION	65
BONUS MATERIALS: All bonus materials can be downloaded by scanning the QR Code below.	69
Appendix A – Emergency Family Survival Plan	71
Appendix B – Financial Collapse Checklist	73
Appendix C – Excel Tracker (Budget & Inventory Sheet)	75
Appendix D – Emergency Family Survival Plan (Printable Template)	77
Appendix E – Financial Collapse Checklist (One-Page Quick Reference)	79
Appendix F – Excel Tracker (Budget & Inventory Sheet for Prepping Supplies)	81
Acknowledgments	83
About the Author	85

INTRODUCTION

WHY THIS BOOK MATTERS NOW: THE REAL RISK OF A DOLLAR COLLAPSE.

For over a century, the U.S. dollar has been more than just money—it has been the heartbeat of American life. Paychecks, savings accounts, mortgages, retirement plans, even international trade—all of it has depended on the strength of the dollar. It has served as the world's reserve currency, a symbol of power, and the backbone of prosperity. When Americans traveled abroad, they carried confidence in their wallets because the dollar was trusted everywhere.

But history teaches us a hard truth: no currency, no matter how powerful, is immune to collapse. The Roman denarius once ruled the known world. The British pound sterling was the global standard for centuries. Both eventually fell. Today, cracks are forming in the dollar's foundation.

Inflation is eating away at paychecks. America's national debt has soared past levels once thought unimaginable. Meanwhile, global powers like China, Russia, and the BRICS nations are openly working to challenge the dollar's dominance, building trade systems that bypass it entirely. These aren't distant warnings—they are happening now.

For the first time in living memory, the question is no longer *if* the dollar could collapse, but *when*. And when it does, it won't be politicians or bankers who pay the price—it will be ordinary Americans. It will be families, workers, retirees, and small businesses that feel the shock first.

This book exists because ignoring the risk is no longer an option. Hoping it never happens is not a strategy. You need knowledge, tools, and a plan—not next year, not when it's too late, but right now.

WHO THIS GUIDE IS FOR: FAMILIES, EVERYDAY AMERICANS, PREPPERS, CAUTIOUS INVESTORS.

Not everyone who picks up this book will consider themselves a "prepper." You don't have to live off the grid, stockpile weapons, or build a bunker to worry about the future of your money. This book is written for ordinary people who sense that something isn't right—and who want to take action before it's too late.

• **Families** who want to make sure their children are safe if the system falters. Parents don't need another lecture about politics—they need a clear plan to keep food on the table, the lights on, and stability in their home when chaos spreads outside.

• **Everyday Americans** who feel the squeeze of rising grocery bills and gas prices, and wonder how to stretch a paycheck that no longer stretches far enough. They're not looking for theory; they want real-world steps to survive inflation and protect their households.

• **Preppers** who already stock food, water, and supplies but know that survival isn't just about canned goods and ammunition. They need a financial strategy—how to handle savings, assets, and trade when the dollar collapses.

• **Cautious investors** who worked hard to build retirement accounts, savings, or small businesses, and who now see those lifelines threatened by inflation, debt, and instability. They're not gamblers; they want safe, smart ways to shield their wealth.

This book is for anyone who has ever felt that unease when checking the grocery receipt, watching the national debt climb on the evening news, or hearing foreign leaders openly question the future of the dollar. If you've ever wondered how to safeguard your paycheck, your pantry, and your peace of mind in uncertain times—this guide was written for you.

HOW TO USE THIS BOOK: PRACTICAL STEPS, CHECKLISTS, AND FAMILY ACTION PLANS.

This is not a book of theory—it is a **manual for survival**. You won't find empty predictions, vague warnings, or political speeches here. Instead, every chapter is designed with one goal in mind: to give you the **exact steps** you can take to protect yourself and your family if the dollar falters.

Think of this book as a roadmap. You don't have to read it all at once, and you don't need to be an expert in economics to understand it. Each section breaks down complex problems into **simple, actionable solutions** that you can start using the very same day.

Here's what you'll find inside:

• **Clear explanations of the risks and what they mean for you.** No jargon, no economist's lectures—just plain talk that connects global events to your daily life, so you know why preparation matters.

• **Checklists that turn complex problems into simple actions.** From stocking a pantry to building a cash reserve, these step-by-step lists remove the guesswork and give you a plan you can follow immediately.

- **Family emergency plans you can adapt to your own household.** You'll learn how to assign roles, communicate during a crisis, and keep everyone safe—even if phones, banks, and grocery stores stop working.

- **Financial survival strategies that work whether you have $100 or $100,000 to protect.** Whether you're living paycheck to paycheck or managing significant savings, this book will show you how to guard what you have and make it last.

By the time you finish, you'll have more than just knowledge—you'll have a **step-by-step blueprint** for safeguarding your money, your home, and your loved ones. This isn't about fear. It's about readiness, confidence, and the peace of mind that comes from knowing you are prepared for whatever comes next.

PART I – UNDERSTANDING THE COMING STORM

Every storm begins with signs that most people choose to ignore. The wind shifts, the sky darkens, and yet life goes on as if nothing is wrong—until the storm is suddenly overhead. The same is true of financial collapse. The warning signs are already here: historic inflation, ballooning national debt, global competitors moving away from the dollar, and political leaders who offer no real solutions.

For decades, the U.S. dollar has been seen as invincible—the backbone of the global economy and the guarantee of stability at home. But history teaches us a harsh truth: **no currency lasts forever**. Civilizations rise and fall, and the money that once seemed untouchable becomes worthless paper.

This section of the book is designed to help you see the gathering storm clearly. Before we can prepare, we must understand:

What happens when money dies. - Why the dollar is under attack like never before. - How these shifts will impact ordinary Americans in daily life. - By understanding the storm before it hits, you gain the one advantage that matters most: **time to prepare**.

CHAPTER 1
WHAT HAPPENS WHEN MONEY DIES

MONEY IS NOT JUST PAPER. It is trust—trust that tomorrow a dollar will buy as much as it does today, that your savings will hold their value, and that the system will still function when you wake up in the morning. But history shows us what happens when that trust is broken: money dies, and with it, the illusion of stability.

INFLATION, HYPERINFLATION, AND CURRENCY COLLAPSE IN PLAIN LANGUAGE

Inflation: The Silent Thief

Inflation is like a slow leak in your savings account. You don't notice it immediately, but over time it drains your wealth. A gallon of milk that costs $3 today might cost $3.30 next year. A tank of gas that once cost $40 now takes $50. Wages rarely keep up, which means your paycheck stretches less each month. You can still live, but you start cutting corners—buying cheaper food, postponing repairs, feeling the pressure build quietly. Inflation is often called the "silent tax" because it steals value without most people realizing it until it's too late.

Hyperinflation: When the Dam Breaks

Hyperinflation is inflation on steroids. Instead of prices creeping up by 2–5% a year, they skyrocket by 10%, 50%, even 1,000% in a single year. Imagine that gallon of milk costing $3 in the morning and $5 by evening. Suddenly, people rush to spend their paychecks the second they get them, because waiting even a day makes their money worth less.

Cash becomes trash—literally. People burn bills for heat, use stacks of currency as notepads, or abandon them in the street. In hyperinflation, the very idea of "saving" disappears. Survival becomes a race against time.

Currency Collapse: When Trust is Dead

A currency collapse happens when people no longer believe their nation's money has value. Once that trust is broken, the system unravels at lightning speed. Banks close their doors. ATMs stop working. Savings accounts vanish into thin air. Citizens are forced to improvise, using anything that still holds real value: U.S. dollars (if the collapse happens elsewhere), gold coins, foreign currencies, cigarettes, bags of rice, or even clean water. Money, as we know it, ceases to exist. In its place comes barter, trade, and desperation.

What It Means for Ordinary Americans

When money dies, it doesn't just mean numbers changing on a bank statement. It means panic at the grocery store, where shelves empty faster than they can be restocked. It means chaos at the gas station, where long lines form as people hoard what's left. It means desperation inside living rooms, where parents wonder how to feed their children tomorrow. A currency collapse is not a distant theory—it's a very real human disaster.

LESSONS FROM HISTORY

History is not just about the past—it's a warning. Every generation believes their money is safe, their system unshakable, and their future guaranteed. Yet, time and again, nations that once seemed invincible have watched their currencies collapse into worthlessness. The lessons are written in plain sight.

Weimar Germany (1920s):

After World War I, Germany was drowning in debt and reparations. To cover its obligations, the government printed money endlessly. What followed was one of the most extreme cases of hyperinflation in modern history.

Ordinary people carried **wheelbarrows full of banknotes** just to buy a loaf of bread. By the time they reached the bakery, prices had doubled. Children stacked worthless bills like building blocks and flew them as paper kites. Entire life savings—retirement accounts, pensions, cash hidden under mattresses—vanished in a matter of months.

The lesson: once a government loses control of its currency, recovery is nearly impossible without total collapse.

Argentina (1990s–2000s):

For decades, Argentina was considered one of the most prosperous nations in South America. But years of debt, corruption, and bad policies led to repeated currency crises.

Families woke up to discover their savings accounts frozen or devalued overnight. The middle class, once stable, was forced into survival mode. People bartered clothing, electronics, and even family heirlooms just to buy food. Shops refused pesos and demanded U.S. dollars or foreign currency instead.

The lesson: even in a modern, educated society, collapse comes suddenly and brutally—turning teachers, doctors, and shopkeepers into barter traders overnight.

Venezuela (2010s–2020s):

Venezuela was once the richest country in Latin America, blessed with the world's largest oil reserves. But decades of mismanagement and corruption led to runaway hyperinflation.

Salaries became worthless in days. Workers were paid billions of bolivars, only to discover the money couldn't buy a carton of eggs. Shoppers carried bags of cash to the market, only to have vendors refuse it. Instead, people demanded U.S. dollars, gold jewelry, or even food staples like rice and sugar. Crime surged, hunger spread, and millions fled the country in desperation.

The lesson: wealth and resources mean nothing when trust in the currency is lost. Even a nation overflowing with oil collapsed when its money became meaningless.

The Warning for America

History proves that no nation, however strong, is immune. The collapse is always **faster and more brutal** than expected. One day people laugh at the possibility. The next, they wake up to empty ATMs, soaring prices, and paychecks that can't buy groceries.

The only difference between nations that survive and those that crumble is whether ordinary citizens prepare before the storm.

THE MOST DANGEROUS MYTH: "IT CAN'T HAPPEN HERE"

If there is one phrase that blinds Americans to the danger ahead, it is this: *"It can't happen here."*

We hear it from politicians who promise that America is too powerful to fail. We hear it from neighbors who shrug off warnings about inflation or debt. We even tell it to ourselves when we feel uneasy about rising prices at the store. The belief is comforting—but deadly.

The truth is that every empire in history thought the same thing.

• **Rome** believed its legions and wealth would keep it invincible—until corruption and overspending hollowed it out from within.

• **Britain** once ruled the seas and the global financial system with the pound sterling as the world's reserve currency. Today, that dominance is a memory.

• **Germany** in the early 20th century was an industrial powerhouse, yet within a decade it descended into hyperinflation and chaos.

And now, America stands on the same edge—**drowning in debt, printing trillions of dollars, and facing global rivals who openly plot to dethrone the dollar.**

The myth that "it can't happen here" is what keeps people unprepared. It lulls families into leaving their savings unprotected, convinces workers that their pensions are secure, and tricks investors into believing that the system will always reset itself. But when trust in money breaks, collapse comes faster than anyone expects.

By the time reality sets in—when the banks close, when the grocery shelves empty, when your dollars buy almost nothing—it will already be too late to start preparing.

The wisest course is not to assume America is immune, but to learn from history and act before the storm arrives.

CHAPTER 2
THE DOLLAR UNDER ATTACK

FOR NEARLY 80 YEARS, the U.S. dollar has been the center of the global financial system. It is the currency used in international trade, the standard for oil and energy, and the storehouse of wealth for foreign governments. But that dominance is now being challenged—and the cracks are widening every day.

THE THREAT OF DE-DOLLARIZATION

For decades, the world had no alternative to the dollar. Whether you were in Europe, Asia, or Africa, global trade revolved around the greenback. But today, rising powers are working together to break that dependence.

- **BRICS nations (Brazil, Russia, India, China, South Africa)** are building new systems of trade that bypass the dollar entirely. They are pushing for a common currency and increasing their use of local currencies in international deals.

- **Oil and energy deals**—once always priced in dollars—are now being signed in Chinese yuan, Russian rubles, and even barter arrangements. The petrodollar system, which has long supported America's strength, is under threat.

- **Rising gold reserves:** Central banks across the globe are buying gold at record levels. Why? Because they no longer trust the dollar to hold its value in the long term. Gold is the ultimate hedge against a collapsing currency.

The move toward de-dollarization is not a theory—it's happening right now. Every time a major trade deal is signed outside the dollar, the foundations of America's financial power weaken.

AMERICA'S DEBT SPIRAL AND THE FEDERAL RESERVE'S ROLE

While foreign nations are working to undermine the dollar from the outside, America is quietly sabotaging itself from the inside. The United States now carries **over $30 trillion in national debt**—a number so large it is almost impossible for the average citizen to grasp. Imagine stacking $1 bills: $30 trillion would stretch far enough to circle the Earth more than 100 times. That is how deep the hole has become.

To keep the system afloat, the government doesn't cut spending—it borrows more. Year after year, Washington raises the debt ceiling, spends trillions it doesn't have, and pushes the problem further down the road. To cover the shortfall, it turns to the Federal Reserve, America's central bank, which has one solution for every crisis: print more money.

The Federal Reserve's policies—**artificially low interest rates, quantitative easing, and endless bailouts**—have flooded the world with dollars. In the short term, these measures act like morphine for a wounded patient: they numb the pain and keep the economy staggering forward. But in the long run, they weaken the body until collapse is inevitable.

Every new dollar created out of thin air reduces the value of the dollars already in your wallet. It's like watering down a pot of soup. At first, you can barely tell. But keep adding water, and eventually all that's left is a tasteless broth with no substance. That's what inflation is doing to your paycheck, your savings, and your retirement account.

And the world is paying attention. Foreign governments see America's addiction to debt and easy money, and they are asking the question nobody in Washington dares to face: *Why should we trust the dollar when America itself doesn't respect it?*

The uncomfortable truth is that America has entered a **debt spiral**—a cycle in which borrowing, printing, and spending feed one another, making escape nearly impossible. At some point, the spiral no longer slows down. It accelerates. And when that happens, the system doesn't just wobble—it breaks.

WHAT THE END OF DOLLAR DOMINANCE MEANS FOR YOUR DAILY LIFE

For most Americans, the idea of a dollar collapse feels abstract—something that happens in far-off countries with unstable governments, not in the United States. But if the dollar loses its position as the world's reserve currency, the consequences here at home will be immediate and brutal. This isn't a distant possibility—it's a direct threat to your grocery bill, your gas tank, your paycheck, and your future.

Soaring Prices

Everyday goods that most families take for granted—electronics, clothing, coffee, even the food on your dinner table—would suddenly become luxury items. Why? Because the U.S. imports much of what it consumes, and if foreign nations stop accepting cheap dollars, they will demand stronger currencies or gold instead. The result: the cost of a $900 laptop could shoot to $2,000. A $10 bag of groceries could jump to $25. Inflation wouldn't creep anymore—it would explode.

Gas and Energy Costs

If oil is no longer traded in dollars, America's energy security collapses overnight. Gasoline at the pump could double or triple within weeks. Imagine paying $10 or even $15 a gallon to fill your tank. Heating your home in the winter or running air conditioning in the summer could suddenly be out of reach for millions. And when energy prices rise, *everything else* —transportation, shipping, farming—becomes more expensive too.

Savings Wiped Out

Most Americans trust that their retirement accounts, pensions, or savings will be there when they need them. But if the dollar collapses, the numbers in your account may not matter. A $100,000 retirement fund might buy only a year's worth of groceries. Pensions could shrink to nothing. Decades of hard work and saving could be erased in a matter of months.

Declining Standard of Living

The American lifestyle—cheap goods, global power, and financial stability—depends entirely on dollar dominance. If that dominance disappears, so does the standard of living we've known for generations. Families would downsize homes, skip medical care, cut meals, and delay every purchase. Millions who once considered themselves middle class could find themselves in poverty, overnight.

This isn't speculation. This is exactly what happened to **Argentina**, where a professional class was forced into bartering groceries. It happened in **Venezuela**, where salaries became worthless and food shortages sparked riots. The only difference is that America's collapse would not just shake one nation—it would send shockwaves through the entire global system. And when that happens, ordinary American families—people like you—will feel the shock first.

The dollar is under attack from both outside and inside. If America loses its financial dominance, life as we know it will change forever. The time to prepare is not when the collapse begins—but now, while you still have the chance.

PART II – PROTECTING YOUR WEALTH

When a storm threatens, the first instinct is to protect what matters most. In a financial collapse, that means safeguarding your wealth—not just in banks or numbers on a screen, but in real, tangible forms that hold value no matter what happens to the dollar.

History proves that when currencies fail, those who survive are not the ones who trusted the system blindly, but the ones who prepared. Gold, silver, land, and barter items have always outlasted collapsing money. At the same time, smart strategies—keeping cash reserves, diversifying assets, and planning for both real and digital risks—can mean the difference between despair and stability.

This part of the book is your step-by-step guide to protecting what you have, whether it's $100 or $100,000. You'll learn how to convert fragile paper wealth into lasting security, how to choose assets that hold value when dollars don't, and how to build a financial survival plan that your family can rely on in the toughest times.

The goal isn't just to survive the collapse—it's to **outlast it and come out stronger on the other side.**

CHAPTER 3
HARD ASSETS THAT HOLD VALUE

WHEN PAPER MONEY COLLAPSES, history shows us one undeniable truth: **real assets survive.** Unlike printed dollars, they cannot be inflated away, erased by a keystroke, or dismissed by government decree. They hold value because people can see them, touch them, and use them. In times of crisis, trust shifts from numbers in a bank account to **hard, tangible assets**.

GOLD, SILVER, AND PRECIOUS METALS: PROS, CONS, AND PRACTICAL STORAGE

For centuries, **gold and silver have been the ultimate hedge against collapsing currencies.** When empires fell and paper money became worthless, those who held precious metals could still trade, barter, and protect their families. Unlike fiat currency, metals cannot be printed at will by governments. They are **rare, durable, and universally recognized.** That's why central banks around the world are stockpiling them even today—they know that when confidence fails, gold and silver endure.

Pros of Precious Metals

- **Accepted worldwide as money.** No matter where you go, gold and silver are trusted. A gold coin is as valuable in New York as it is in Zurich or Tokyo.

- **Portable and easily divisible.** Gold bars are ideal for storing large amounts of wealth, while silver coins can be traded for small, everyday needs. Silver especially works well for "change" in a barter economy.

- **A proven store of value.** For over 5,000 years, gold and silver have outlasted kings, empires, and entire financial systems. When paper currencies died, precious metals remained.

Cons of Precious Metals

- **Not easily spendable in everyday transactions.** You won't be able to buy milk at Walmart with a gold coin. Precious metals are best as a backup store of value, not a daily currency.

- **Short-term price fluctuations.** In times of crisis, the value of gold and silver can swing wildly, especially on paper markets. This can cause panic among those who don't understand the long-term strength of metals.

- **Storage and security are critical.** Gold and silver are tempting targets for thieves. If not properly stored, your hedge could disappear overnight.

Practical Storage Tips

- **Keep some small silver coins** on hand. Pre-1965 U.S. quarters and dimes, often called *"junk silver"*, contain 90% silver and are perfect for barter. These coins are instantly recognizable, hard to counterfeit, and easy to trade for food or supplies.

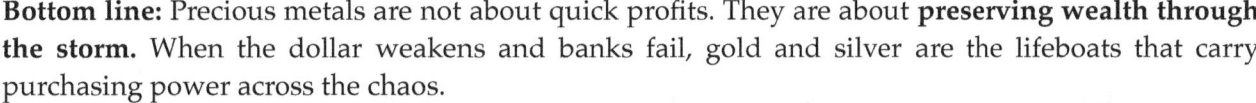

- **Store larger amounts safely.** A fireproof home safe bolted to the floor, or a private vault (not tied to banks) are best. Remember: in a crisis, banks can close, seize deposits, or restrict withdrawals. Don't let your metals get trapped behind locked doors you don't control.

- **Avoid ETFs or "paper gold."** Precious metals traded on Wall Street are not the same as physical metals in your hand. If you can't touch it, you don't own it. In a collapse, paper gold may become as worthless as the dollars it's priced in.

- **Diversify storage.** Don't keep all your metals in one place. A mix of home storage, private vaults, and small hidden caches ensures you're not wiped out by theft or seizure.

Bottom line: Precious metals are not about quick profits. They are about **preserving wealth through the storm.** When the dollar weakens and banks fail, gold and silver are the lifeboats that carry purchasing power across the chaos.

FARMLAND, REAL ESTATE, AND TANGIBLE GOODS

Another class of hard assets that consistently outlasts paper money is **land and property**. Unlike dollars—which can be printed, devalued, or inflated away—land produces **real value**: food, shelter, and rental income. In every major collapse in history, farmland has proven to be one of the most secure and practical investments, because no matter how bad things get, people will always need food.

• • •

Farmland

Farmland is more than an investment—it is survival. A few acres of fertile soil can provide:

- **Crops** that feed your family and can be traded with neighbors.

- **Livestock** for meat, milk, and eggs. Chickens, goats, and rabbits can turn grass and feed into protein and barter items.

- **A sustainable source of income or barter goods**, even in the worst economic downturn.

In places like the American Midwest, farmland values have remained relatively stable even when housing markets crashed. In fact, during crises, farmland often increases in value because food security becomes priceless. For those unable to purchase large tracts, even **community gardens, leased plots, or backyard homesteads** can become survival lifelines.

Real Estate

Not all real estate is equal in times of crisis. Property in crowded urban centers may lose value quickly as crime rises, services fail, and populations flee to safer areas. On the other hand, **rural and suburban properties** often become highly desirable because they offer space, safety, and independence.

- **Suburban homes with land** allow families to grow food and live away from unrest.

- **Rural cabins or homesteads** can serve as long-term retreats during instability.

- **Multi-family units in stable regions** may continue to provide rental income, especially if tenants pay in barter or alternative currencies.

The key lesson: in a collapse, real estate tied to **self-reliance** will thrive, while property tied only to **luxury or convenience** will collapse in value.

Tangible Goods

Beyond land, **practical equipment and durable goods** can become more valuable than cash when supply chains break down. Items that produce energy, clean water, or food are not luxuries—they are lifelines.

- A **chainsaw** can clear land, cut firewood, and help build shelters.

- A **water filter** may literally save lives when clean water becomes scarce.

- A **solar panel** can power radios, lights, and small appliances when the grid goes down.

- **Hand tools, seeds, fishing gear, and hunting equipment** all hold immense barter value in a survival economy.

During normal times, these items may seem ordinary. But in crisis, a gallon of fuel, a working generator, or a box of nails could be worth far more than stacks of paper dollars.

The Lesson

The principle is simple: **owning something real and useful will always outweigh relying on something digital and fragile.** Farmland, rural property, and durable tools are assets that serve your family directly while also functioning as trade goods in a failing economy. Unlike a number on a bank statement, these assets produce, protect, and provide in any scenario.

EVERYDAY BARTER ITEMS

In a true collapse, when confidence in the dollar evaporates, communities often return to the oldest form of trade: **barter.** Gold and silver may protect long-term wealth, but in the middle of a crisis, they are not what keeps families fed and safe. Instead, it's the **small, everyday items**—things that solve immediate problems—that become the "currency" of survival.

When stores are empty, supply chains broken, and banks closed, a simple bar of soap, a pack of batteries, or a gallon of fuel can be worth more than paper money. These items carry value because they provide comfort, security, or survival in the moment.

Alcohol

Whiskey, vodka, and even small bottles of wine become highly desirable in hard times. Alcohol can be used for relaxation, as a disinfectant, or as a universal trade item. Small bottles are especially valuable because they are easy to store and trade in small amounts.

Tobacco and Cigarettes

For smokers, these are not luxuries but necessities. In past crises, cigarettes have been used as currency—so much so that during World War II, they were more trusted than local money in parts of Europe.

Ammunition and Firearms Accessories

In rural America, where hunting and self-defense are part of daily life, ammunition can be more valuable than gold. A box of 9mm rounds or shotgun shells could become one of the most sought-after trade items in a collapse scenario.

Batteries, Flashlights, and Candles

When the power grid fails, light becomes a survival tool. Batteries, flashlights, headlamps, and candles can restore safety and comfort. Even in modern blackouts, these items sell out instantly.

Soap, Hygiene Products, and Medicine

Cleanliness is survival. Soap, toothpaste, deodorant, and basic hygiene supplies will be worth their weight in silver. Medicine—especially antibiotics, pain relievers, and first aid supplies—can be priceless when hospitals are overwhelmed or inaccessible.

Food Staples

Rice, beans, sugar, salt, flour, and canned goods are the foundation of survival. They are cheap today, but in a collapse, they become the most valuable barter items because they provide direct sustenance. A 50-pound bag of rice could feed a family for weeks—or buy tools, fuel, or services in trade.

Fuel

Propane, kerosene, and gasoline stored safely in containers will be worth more than cash when pumps run dry. Fuel powers generators, vehicles, heaters, and even cooking equipment. Without it, modern life grinds to a halt.

The Harsh Truth

In desperate times, **the ability to trade a bar of soap, a bag of rice, or a bottle of whiskey may keep your family alive.** These are the kinds of small, practical items that hold value when the dollar does not. While it may seem strange to imagine trading candles or canned beans for services, history shows this is exactly what happens when economies collapse. The key is to **think small, stock practical, and store wisely.**

CHAPTER 4
DIGITAL ASSETS AND MODERN RISKS

FOR MANY AMERICANS, the rise of Bitcoin and other digital assets has been a promise of freedom from the traditional financial system. "Digital gold," "borderless money," and "decentralized banking" are phrases that have fueled a movement of people seeking security outside of the dollar. But while cryptocurrencies and digital finance offer opportunities, they also come with vulnerabilities that few investors want to face.

BITCOIN AND CRYPTOCURRENCIES: OPPORTUNITIES VS. VULNERABILITIES

Over the past decade, Bitcoin has gone from an obscure experiment in digital money to a trillion-dollar global phenomenon. For many Americans—especially younger generations disillusioned with Wall Street and government debt—cryptocurrencies seem like the future of freedom and financial independence. But while there are undeniable opportunities, there are also serious risks that every family, investor, and prepper must understand.

☑ Opportunities

Decentralization

One of the biggest appeals of Bitcoin is that it isn't controlled by Washington, Wall Street, or any central bank. Instead, it runs on a decentralized global network, maintained by thousands of independent "miners" and computers worldwide. For people concerned about inflation, bailouts, or government corruption, this makes Bitcoin feel like a lifeboat outside the traditional system.

Portability

Unlike gold or real estate, Bitcoin is weightless. A small flash drive or even a 12-word "seed phrase" memorized in your head can hold millions of dollars' worth of value. In countries like Argentina or Ukraine, people have literally walked across borders with their life savings stored digitally—safe from confiscation or devaluation. For Americans worried about banking freezes or capital controls, this is a powerful advantage.

Global Use

Unlike cash, which can be limited by borders or exchange rates, Bitcoin can move across the world in minutes. Whether you're sending value from Texas to Tokyo or New York to Nairobi, the transaction bypasses banks, wire fees, and government oversight. In a future where the dollar is challenged, this global acceptance could make Bitcoin a lifeline for cross-border trade.

⚠ Vulnerabilities

Volatility

The very feature that makes cryptocurrencies exciting—their independence from traditional finance—is also what makes them unstable. Bitcoin has lost more than 80% of its value in past crashes, only to rebound later. For families relying on savings, this means wealth can evaporate overnight. In a survival scenario, such swings can make digital assets unreliable as your primary store of value.

Hacks and Scams

For every story of Bitcoin millionaires, there are countless stories of people losing everything. Billions of dollars have been stolen through hacked exchanges, phishing emails, and fraudulent "altcoin" schemes. Unlike banks, there is no FDIC insurance in crypto. If your exchange goes bankrupt or if you misplace your password, your money is simply gone—forever.

Dependency on Infrastructure

Perhaps the greatest vulnerability of all: Bitcoin requires electricity, internet, and functioning digital networks to exist. In a world where cyberattacks, EMPs, or rolling blackouts are real threats, digital wealth can vanish into inaccessibility in seconds. During the Venezuelan blackouts of the 2010s, crypto wallets became useless. People who thought they were safe suddenly had nothing to trade for food or medicine.

The Bottom Line

Bitcoin and other cryptocurrencies can play a role in protecting wealth outside of the traditional system—but they cannot replace **tangible, physical assets** in a survival plan. They are tools, not foundations. Smart investors may hold some digital assets, but wise survivalists will never rely on them alone.

STABLECOINS AND THE RISK OF GOVERNMENT CRACKDOWNS

Stablecoins—digital tokens designed to mimic the value of the U.S. dollar—are often advertised as the "safe middle ground" between volatile cryptocurrencies and traditional cash. On the surface, they seem perfect: one token equals one dollar, easy to send across borders, usable in digital wallets, and often faster than PayPal or bank wires. For millions of people worldwide, especially in unstable economies like Argentina, Nigeria, and Turkey, stablecoins have become a lifeline against local currency collapse.

But beneath the surface lies a dangerous truth: stablecoins are **only as strong as the dollar and the private companies that issue them.** Unlike Bitcoin, which operates on decentralized math and code, stablecoins depend on trust—trust that the issuer actually holds enough reserves, trust that governments will allow them to operate, and trust that the peg will never break.

! **The Hidden Risks**

• **Government Power**: Stablecoins can be frozen, regulated, or outlawed overnight. The same governments that control banks can—and already have—pressured stablecoin issuers to block accounts, restrict transfers, or hand over data. If Washington decides stablecoins are a threat to financial stability, they could disappear with the stroke of a pen.

• **Fragile Backing**: Many issuers claim they have "dollars in reserve" for every token. But audits and investigations have shown that some are backed not by cash, but by risky debt or commercial paper. If investors panic and rush to withdraw, the collapse could resemble a digital bank run, wiping out billions instantly.

• **The CBDC Threat**: With Central Bank Digital Currencies (CBDCs) on the horizon, the U.S. government may one day **replace stablecoins entirely** with a state-controlled digital dollar. Unlike stablecoins, CBDCs would give Washington total visibility and control over every transaction—something many Americans deeply fear.

Stablecoins are useful tools, but they are **not untouchable.** If you rely on them, you are still betting on trust—trust in corporations, trust in audits, and trust in governments that may decide to shut them down when it suits their agenda. History shows that every new form of money eventually faces regulation, control, or collapse. Believing that "this time is different" is the most dangerous gamble of all.

WHY ELECTRICITY AND INTERNET BLACKOUTS COULD ERASE DIGITAL WEALTH OVERNIGHT

When people imagine financial collapse, they often think of numbers on screens losing value. But what if the screen itself goes dark? Imagine a massive cyberattack targeting U.S. banks, a coordinated EMP strike, or even a Category 5 hurricane ripping through power lines. In a moment, the grid fails. The internet is gone. Your phone won't connect. ATMs are dead. Even credit card readers at the grocery store are useless.

In that moment, what good is Bitcoin, Ethereum, or any digital coin? You can't transfer it, you can't sell it, you can't even prove you own it without access to the internet. Unlike gold in your hand or a bag of rice in your pantry, digital wealth vanishes the second electricity disappears.

This isn't theoretical—it has already happened. In Venezuela, recurring nationwide blackouts turned crypto wallets into dead weight. Citizens who once used Bitcoin for daily transactions were forced back into barter, U.S. cash, and gold jewelry. A similar story unfolded in Puerto Rico after Hurricane Maria, when months of outages left people unable to use digital banking at all.

The brutal truth is simple: **digital assets are not physical.** You can't eat them, burn them for heat, or trade them for bread at the farmer's market during a blackout. They may serve as part of a long-term wealth strategy, but they cannot be your primary lifeline in a crisis.

Digital assets can **diversify** wealth and provide opportunities in a global, connected world. But in collapse scenarios, they are only as strong as the grid that sustains them. A wise survivalist may keep some Bitcoin—but never without also holding **tangible goods, precious metals, and practical supplies** that will still hold value when the lights go out.

CHAPTER 5
DIVERSIFYING YOUR FINANCIAL SURVIVAL

CHAPTER 5: **Diversifying Your Financial Survival**

When facing the threat of a dollar collapse, there is no single "magic bullet" asset that will save you. Gold alone won't feed your family. Cryptocurrencies won't keep you warm during a blackout. And holding stacks of cash under your mattress won't protect you from inflation. True resilience comes from **diversification**—spreading your wealth across multiple forms so that no single crisis wipes you out.

Just as investors build balanced portfolios for normal times, survivalists must build **financial survival portfolios** for hard times. The key is to balance **liquidity (spending power today)** with **durability (wealth that will hold value tomorrow).**

CASH ON HAND: HOW MUCH AND IN WHAT DENOMINATIONS

In an emergency, **cash is king—at least for a while.** Even in the middle of a currency crisis, there is usually a **transition period** where people continue to accept paper dollars out of habit and necessity. That brief window may be your lifeline.

Imagine this: the power grid is down, ATMs have gone dark, and stores hang signs reading *"Cash Only."* If you've prepared by keeping physical bills, you can still buy food, fill your gas tank, or pay a handyman to fix your generator. But if your wealth exists only in bank accounts or digital wallets, you may be locked out entirely.

◆ **Small Denominations Matter Most**

Many people make the mistake of hoarding stacks of $100 bills. But in a survival scenario, **big bills are often useless.**

- A gas station clerk without change will refuse your $100 bill for $15 worth of gas.

- A small-town grocer may not risk breaking it when counterfeits are on the rise.
- Neighbors you want to trade with will prefer small, exact payments.

That's why **$1s, $5s, $10s, and $20s are your real survival currency.** They are practical, easy to trade, and harder to counterfeit in small transactions.

Think of it this way: if society slows down to a cash-only economy, it will run more like a flea market than a shopping mall. You'll want plenty of "small change."

◆ Building Your Emergency Stash

Experts recommend keeping at least **two weeks of living expenses in cash** safely stored at home. For most families, that means **$500 to $2,000** depending on your household size and budget.

- **Solo survivalist** → $500–$700 may cover gas, groceries, and basic supplies.
- **Small family** → $1,000–$1,500 helps secure food, fuel, and emergency repairs.
- **Larger household** → $2,000 or more provides flexibility for unexpected costs.

Remember: in a crisis, cash is not about luxury purchases—it's about keeping your family fed, mobile, and safe.

◆ Hiding It Wisely

Where you keep your cash is as important as how much you keep. A visible envelope in your drawer won't cut it when looters, burglars, or even desperate neighbors come looking.

Smart storage ideas include:

- A **fireproof safe** bolted to the floor.
- **Hidden compartments** in furniture or household items (false-bottom drawers, hollowed-out books, behind wall plates).
- **Multiple stashes**—don't keep it all in one place. If one hiding spot is discovered, you won't lose everything.
- **Decoy wallets** with a small amount of cash to hand over in case of robbery.

The goal is to make your emergency stash both **accessible to you** and **invisible to others.**

◆ The Reality of Cash in Collapse

Cash won't last forever. If hyperinflation hits, your stack of bills will buy less every day. Eventually, people will prefer goods, gold, or foreign currencies.

But in the **first days and weeks of panic**, nothing beats paper money for quick, practical exchanges. **It bridges the gap** between normal life and full survival mode—giving you precious time to adapt while others scramble.

☑ **The Takeaway**: Treat cash as your **first line of defense**, not your ultimate plan. It buys you time to secure food, fuel, and stability before the system unravels.

FOREIGN CURRENCIES AS BACKUP

When the dollar falters, survival often depends on whether you can trade in something people still trust. Around the world, during times of economic collapse, those who had access to foreign currencies often managed to buy food, fuel, and medicine long after their national money became worthless.

Why Foreign Currencies Matter

Most people think of foreign currency as something only travelers or businesses need. But in a collapse, strong currencies become lifelines. They act as a bridge between the dying dollar and whatever new system emerges. Even small amounts can make the difference between getting supplies or going without.

Key Options

- **The Euro & Swiss Franc**: Historically seen as stable, these currencies tend to hold value when others fall. The Swiss Franc in particular is often considered a "safe haven" in global finance.

- **The Canadian Dollar**: For Americans living near the northern border, Canadian cash could remain highly practical. If trade across the border continues, it may be accepted in local markets or by individuals looking for alternatives to the dollar.

- **Other Trusted Currencies**: Japanese Yen and British Pounds may also provide backup value, especially in larger cities with international connections.

Practical Advantages

- **Hard-to-Fake Cash**: Many foreign currencies use advanced anti-counterfeiting designs, making them more reliable in black-market exchanges.

- **Portability**: A few hundred dollars' worth in foreign notes can fit easily in a wallet or small envelope, providing discreet security.

- **Liquidity in Crisis**: Unlike precious metals, which may require finding the right buyer, foreign bills can often be spent directly with little negotiation.

Even a few hundred dollars in foreign currency tucked away at home could provide crucial backup if U.S. cash becomes worthless overnight. Think of it not as an investment, but as **insurance**—something you hope you'll never need, but will be glad you have if the system cracks.

BALANCING REAL VS. DIGITAL WEALTH FOR MAXIMUM RESILIENCE

When preparing for a dollar crisis, the worst mistake you can make is betting everything on a single strategy. No single asset is perfect. Each one shines in certain conditions but fails in others. True resilience comes from balance—layering your survival wealth across **real, cash, and digital assets** so you are never left empty-handed.

Strengths and Weaknesses:

- **Gold & Precious Metals**: Timeless stores of value, but not practical for buying bread at the corner store.

- **Cash & Currency**: Essential in the opening weeks of chaos, but rapidly eaten away by inflation.

- **Cryptocurrencies & Digital Assets**: Borderless and portable, but only as strong as the internet and electricity grid that sustain them.

The Layered Approach to Survival Wealth

Survivalists must think in **time horizons**, preparing for each stage of collapse differently:

1 Day 1–30: Immediate Survival: Cash in small bills for groceries, gas, and essentials when banks are offline. - Food stockpiles and barter items (soap, alcohol, batteries). - Small silver coins ("junk silver") for quick, trusted exchanges.

2 Month 1–12: Stabilizing the Family: Silver and gold for preserving purchasing power. - Foreign currencies (Euros, Swiss Francs, Canadian Dollars) to navigate cross-border trade or black markets. - Tangible goods like generators, water filters, and farming tools that hold real, practical value.

3 Year 1 and Beyond: Rebuilding & Sustainability: Real estate and farmland as long-term anchors of security. - Livestock, gardens, and renewable energy sources that reduce dependency on broken systems. - Carefully managed digital wealth—like Bitcoin—for potential future opportunities if global trade adapts online.

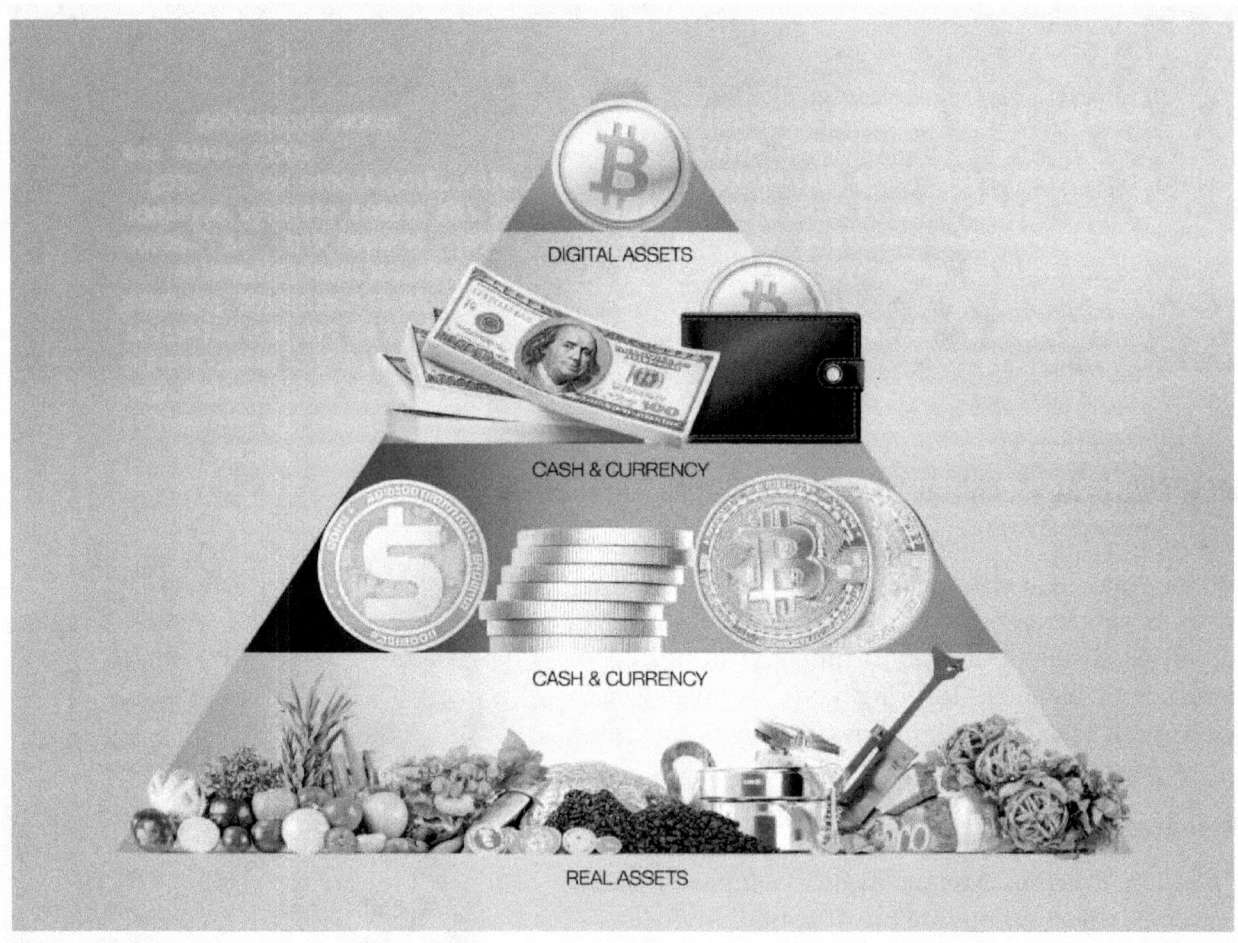

Diversification isn't about chasing profits—it's about **insurance for survival**. Think of your wealth not as numbers on a screen, but as **layers of defense** around your family. If one layer fails, the others step in. With this tiered strategy, you won't just endure the first shockwaves—you'll have the foundation to adapt and even thrive in whatever comes next.

✅ **The Lesson:** True financial preparedness is not about getting rich—it's about ensuring that no matter what stage of collapse arrives, your family can still eat, trade, and live with dignity.

PART III – SURVIVAL BEYOND MONEY

When dollars, banks, and digital systems fail, survival is no longer about wealth—it's about resilience. This part of the book shifts focus from finances to the essentials of life: food, water, shelter, security, and community. Money can vanish, but the skills you practice, the tools you own, and the plans you make will determine whether your family endures the crisis or becomes a victim of it.

In these chapters, you'll learn how to secure clean water, store long-term food, create safe shelter, defend your home, and build a trusted network of allies. This is the stage where survival moves beyond banknotes and balance sheets into the realm of true independence.

CHAPTER 6
WHEN DOLLARS CAN'T BUY BREAD

WHEN A CURRENCY COLLAPSES, money loses its meaning. No matter how many bills you hold, if store shelves are empty or merchants refuse paper dollars, you cannot eat them. Survival shifts from having money to having what money was supposed to buy—food, water, medicine, and the skills to produce them.

BUILDING A 30–90 DAY FOOD RESERVE

When panic strikes, grocery stores become war zones. During hurricanes, blizzards, or even short-term supply chain shocks, shelves have been stripped bare in hours. Now imagine that scenario stretched for weeks—or months. In an economic collapse, restocking becomes uncertain or even impossible. That's why building a reliable food reserve is not a luxury—it's a necessity.

Start Small, Build Steady

Don't let the idea of storing three months of food overwhelm you. Begin with one week's worth of meals your family already eats. Once that feels manageable, expand to 30 days, then 60, and finally 90. By growing steadily, you spread out the cost and avoid waste. This gradual method also allows you to learn which foods your household actually uses and enjoys.

Choose Long-Lasting Foods

Some foods spoil quickly, but others can last for years when stored properly. Focus on staples that are:

- **Calorie-dense** (rice, beans, pasta, oats, peanut butter).

- **Nutrient-rich** (lentils, canned fish, dried fruit, powdered milk).
- **Shelf-stable** (canned vegetables, tomato paste, cooking oil).
- **Flexible in recipes** (rice and beans can be combined with almost anything).

➡ Example: A 20-pound bag of rice can feed a family for weeks and costs less than a single dinner out. A flat of canned vegetables provides essential vitamins when fresh produce is scarce.

Rotate and Replace

Your food reserve is not a "buy it and forget it" investment. Use the "first in, first out" rule: eat the oldest items first, replace them with new purchases, and always keep your stockpile fresh. This way, your reserve is never wasted—it simply becomes part of your normal grocery cycle.

Don't Forget Comfort Foods

Survival isn't only physical—it's psychological. Small luxuries like coffee, tea, sugar, honey, spices, or chocolate can lift morale in stressful times. In fact, these items often carry **high barter value**, making them both comforting and practical.

Storage Tips

- Store food in cool, dry places away from sunlight.
- Use airtight containers, buckets with gamma lids, or vacuum-sealed bags for bulk goods.
- Label containers with purchase and expiration dates for easy rotation.
- Keep a mix of ready-to-eat foods (like canned chili or tuna) and cook-required staples (like rice and beans).

✅ **The Goal**: A three-month buffer means you won't be forced into panic buying when shelves are empty or into risky barter situations with desperate neighbors. It gives your family stability when chaos reigns outside.

90-Day Food Reserve Checklist (Family of 4)

Grains & Staples
- Rice: 100–120 lbs
- Pasta: 60–80 lbs
- Oats: 30–40 lbs
- Flour: 50 lbs

Fats & Oils
- Cooking Oil (olive, vegetable, or coconut): 6–8 gallons
- Ghee or Shelf-Stable Butter: 10–15 lbs

Proteins
- Beans (dried): 60–70 lbs
- Lentils: 40 lbs
- Peanut Butter: 12–15 jars
- Canned Meat (tuna, chicken, beef, salmon): 90–120 cans

Fruits & Vegetables
- Canned Vegetables: 90–120 cans
- Canned/Dried Fruit: 60–80 cans/packs
- Tomato Sauce or Paste: 30–40 cans

Dairy Alternatives
- Powdered Milk: 10–15 lbs
- Shelf-Stable Milk or Almond/Soy Milk cartons: 20–30

Extras / Comfort Items
- Coffee: 6–8 lbs
- Tea: 200–300 bags
- Honey or Sugar: 20–30 lbs
- Spices: assorted jars (salt, pepper, garlic powder, chili, etc.)
- Chocolate / Candy: small reserve for morale

Cooking & Miscellaneous
- Instant meals (ramen, mac & cheese, freeze-dried pouches): 30–40 packs
- Baking basics: yeast, baking powder, baking soda
- Vitamins: 3 months' supply per family member

Water & Beverages
- Minimum: 1 gallon per person per day = 360 gallons for 90 days (store in food-grade containers or rotation with bottled water)

WATER, MEDICINE, AND ENERGY AS THE NEW CURRENCIES

When dollars lose value, **essentials replace money**. History shows that in every collapse, those who had stored and protected the basics—water, medicine, and energy—held the real power. These resources become the new currencies of survival, traded and guarded more fiercely than cash.

💧 Water – The First Priority

- **Survival Rule of 3**: You can live 3 weeks without food, 3 days without water, 3 minutes without air.

- **Storage Goal**: At least **1 gallon per person per day** (drinking + cooking + hygiene). For a family of 4, that's **120 gallons per month**.

- **Smart Storage**: Food-grade containers, sealed barrels, or rotating bottled water.

- **Backup Systems**:

  ◦ Portable water filters (LifeStraw, Sawyer Mini).

  ◦ Purification tablets or bleach (unscented).

  ◦ Rainwater catchment systems or gravity-fed filters for long-term resilience.

✅ Checklist – Water

- 120 gallons per month per family of 4
- 2–3 portable water filters
- Purification tablets (minimum 100 doses)
- Bleach (1 gallon, unscented, for disinfection)
- Rainwater catchment barrel or system

💊 Medicine – Health as Wealth

In crisis, pharmacies empty fast. Even small medical supplies become worth more than cash.

- **Core Supplies**:

  ◦ Antibiotics (where legally available) or fish antibiotics as last resort. - Pain relievers: ibuprofen, acetaminophen, aspirin. - Antihistamines: diphenhydramine (Benadryl). - Bandages, gauze, tape, antiseptic wipes. - Multivitamins to prevent deficiencies. - **Hygiene & Sanitation**: Soap, toothpaste, menstrual supplies, hand sanitizer.

- **Natural Remedies**: Honey (antibacterial), garlic (antimicrobial), chamomile (calming), activated charcoal (detox).

✅ Checklist – Medicine

- 3 months' supply of personal prescriptions
- Pain relievers (ibuprofen, acetaminophen)
- First aid kit with bandages & antiseptics
- Antibiotics (if available)
- Multivitamins (90-day supply per person)
- Hygiene kits (soap, toothpaste, feminine products)

⚡ Energy – Power = Survival

When the grid goes down, **energy is wealth**. Without it, food spoils, lights go dark, and safety disappears.

- **Fuel**: Propane tanks, kerosene, gasoline (stored in safe containers with stabilizer).
- **Cooking Alternatives**: Portable camping stoves, rocket stoves, or solar ovens.
- **Electricity Backup**: Solar panels, solar lanterns, rechargeable battery packs, small generators.
- **Heat & Light**: Firewood, candles, oil lamps.

✅ Checklist – Energy

- 2–3 propane tanks (20 lbs each)
- Solar lanterns or crank flashlights
- Small generator with fuel (enough for 1–2 weeks)
- Firewood or alternative heat source
- Power banks for phones & small devices

LEARNING PRACTICAL SKILLS THAT REPLACE MONEY

When a currency loses value, it doesn't just destroy savings—it rewrites the rules of survival. In a collapsed economy, the true measure of wealth is **what you can do**, not what you can spend. Skills become the "currency" that communities trade and rely on.

Picture this: Two families face the same blackout. One has cash tucked away, the other has a father who can repair solar panels and a mother who knows how to preserve vegetables. Which family has leverage? Which one can trade their abilities for food, fuel, or protection?

Here are the most valuable survival skills in a post-dollar world:

- **Gardening & Food Preservation**

Being able to grow your own food—even in small backyard gardens or raised beds—is a shield against empty grocery stores. Add food preservation techniques such as canning, dehydrating, pickling, and fermenting, and you can turn seasonal harvests into year-round security. Raising small livestock like chickens or rabbits adds a renewable source of protein.

- **Medical Knowledge**

When hospitals are overwhelmed or medicine is scarce, the person who knows how to clean wounds, stop bleeding, or treat infections becomes invaluable. Even basic first-aid training—CPR, splinting, disinfecting—turns you into a community lifeline. Stocking medical supplies is crucial, but **knowing how to use them** is what makes them powerful.

- **Mechanical & Repair Skills**

In a world without steady imports, broken equipment doesn't get replaced—it gets fixed. If you can repair a water pump, sharpen tools, or keep a generator running, you'll always have something to trade. Small engine repair, basic carpentry, and solar panel maintenance are worth their weight in gold.

- **Homemade Solutions**

When store shelves are bare, simple products become priceless. The knowledge of how to make soap, candles, vinegar, or natural fire starters can fill the gap. Imagine being the only one in your neighborhood who can provide something as basic as clean soap—it becomes a trade item as valuable as currency.

✅ **The Lesson:** When dollars can't buy bread, survival depends not on the digits in your bank account but on the **skills you've mastered, the food you've grown, and the knowledge you can apply**. Money can vanish in a day. Skills stay with you for life.

CHAPTER 7
SECURITY AND COMMUNITY

WHEN MONEY FAILS, and the system around you begins to break down, danger does not only come from empty shelves or rising prices. It comes from people—fearful, desperate, and sometimes violent—who may see what you have as their survival ticket. At the same time, no single family can endure the storm alone. Security and survival demand both self-reliance and the strength of community.

PROTECTING YOUR HOME AND PROPERTY IN TIMES OF UNREST

In a crisis, your home is more than shelter—it becomes your fortress, your supply depot, and your family's sanctuary. Protecting it doesn't mean living in constant fear, but it does mean having a clear, layered plan for defense. The more prepared you are, the less likely you are to become a target.

- **Layers of Security**

Don't think of security as one wall—it's multiple lines of defense. Imagine concentric circles:

◦ *Outer Layer*: Fencing, thorny bushes under windows, and visible cameras or dummy cameras. Even a "Beware of Dog" sign works as a deterrent.

◦ *Middle Layer*: Solid doors with reinforced locks, shatter-resistant window film, and motion-sensor lighting.

◦ *Inner Layer*: A safe room or designated area inside the house where your family can retreat if a threat breaches the outer layers. Stock it with essentials like a flashlight, phone, first aid kit, and a defensive tool.

- **Deterrence Over Force**

The goal is to avoid conflict, not invite it. Most intruders look for easy targets. If your home appears alert and defended, they are more likely to move on.

◦ Motion-sensor lights and solar-powered garden lights reduce dark hiding spots.

◦ A dog—whether big or small—acts as an alarm system with teeth.

◦ Background noise like a running generator, music, or even a radio talk show suggests the home is occupied and awake.

- **Firearms and Defense Tools**

In desperate times, law enforcement may be stretched thin or absent. Depending on your state laws and personal beliefs, firearms can provide an essential layer of defense. But owning one without training is dangerous.

◦ If you choose this route, invest in professional instruction and regular practice.

◦ Secure storage is critical, especially around children. Quick-access safes are designed for emergencies.

◦ Non-lethal tools like pepper spray, batons, or even heavy-duty flashlights also have a place in your defense plan.

- **Silent Strength**

In survival, sometimes the greatest protection is invisibility.

◦ Never boast about your food stockpile, water reserve, or generator. Word travels fast, and desperate neighbors may remember.

◦ At night, use blackout curtains to keep your home's lighting invisible from the street. A glowing house during a blackout signals supplies inside.

◦ Keep your vehicles fueled and parked in a way that doesn't draw attention to your mobility advantage.

✅ **Remember**: True home security isn't about paranoia—it's about buying time, deterring threats, and creating peace of mind. When your family feels safe, you can focus energy on the bigger survival priorities: food, water, and community.

FORMING LOCAL NETWORKS FOR TRADE AND PROTECTION

When official systems collapse, **local communities become the new economy**. In times of scarcity, isolation is dangerous—while cooperation multiplies security, resources, and resilience. History proves that families who worked together with their neighbors survived better than those who went it alone.

- **Neighborhood Watch with Purpose**

Organize with trusted neighbors, not just for casual watch duty, but for real **mutual defense and awareness**. Simple patrols, rotating shifts, and shared alert systems can make a neighborhood nearly impossible to overwhelm. A single household can be an easy target—but a group of five or ten homes working together sends a clear message: *"This area is not vulnerable."*

- **Barter Circles that Keep Everyone Alive**

Money may die, but value never disappears. Farmers with eggs, mechanics with repair skills, families with extra rice, or someone with medical training can all join a **barter circle**. These micro-economies can meet most needs when supply chains collapse. A small village in Argentina during the 2001 crisis survived almost entirely on community barter clubs—proving this isn't theory, but reality.

- **Skill Sharing as Social Currency**

In a survival economy, **knowledge is wealth**. A nurse's medical training, a carpenter's ability to repair homes, or a hunter's skill in bringing in protein carries as much weight as gold. Encourage open skill-sharing in your network: training sessions, "how-to" workshops, and joint projects. When everyone can contribute, the whole group becomes stronger.

- **Communication Plans Beyond Cell Towers**

When cell phones fail and the internet crashes, communities that already have **alternative communication systems** will stay connected. Walkie-talkies, ham radios, agreed-upon meeting points, or even handwritten notice boards can keep the network informed. A blackout is chaotic for the unprepared—but merely inconvenient for the organized.

☑ **The Takeaway**: In a crisis, your greatest asset isn't gold or guns—it's **trustworthy people**. A strong local network provides both protection and provision, ensuring no one stands alone when survival is on the line.

WHY COMMUNITY RESILIENCE BEATS GOING SOLO

The "lone wolf" survival fantasy may make for an exciting movie, but in real life, it is a dangerous illusion. History and human nature prove that people thrive in groups, not in isolation. When societies collapse, survival is not just about food or weapons—it is about cooperation.

- **Shared Resources**

No single household can store everything. One family might have a well or a water filter, another might raise chickens, while someone else knows herbal medicine. Alone, each is vulnerable. Together, they form a web of resilience that multiplies everyone's chances of survival.

- **Shared Defense**: A lone home is an easy target. But a community with watch schedules, communication systems, and strength in numbers is far less appealing to looters or gangs. A united group can defend with presence and deterrence, not just force.

- **Shared Skills**: A mechanic can repair tools, a nurse can treat wounds, a teacher can educate children, and a gardener can produce food. No one person can master all survival skills, but within a community, every trade has value.

- **Shared Morale**: Survival is not just physical—it's psychological. Isolation breeds fear, despair, and mistakes. Coming together for meals, prayer, or even storytelling restores hope and determination. Emotional strength can carry a group through hardships when supplies alone would not.

☑ **The ultimate truth:** In collapse scenarios, survival is not about clinging to what you have alone—it's about multiplying strength, resources, and hope with others. A resilient community is stronger than any fortress.

CHAPTER 8
THE FINANCIAL SURVIVAL CHECKLIST

WHEN A STORM IS COMING, sailors don't panic—they check their rigging, secure their cargo, and prepare their ship. Financial survival works the same way. Instead of reacting in chaos when the dollar wobbles, you can move step by step through a clear checklist. Think of this as your **blueprint for readiness**—a set of practical, repeatable actions that keep you calm while others scramble.

This is not theory. It's your **hands-on survival plan**.

STEP 1: SECURE ESSENTIAL ASSETS

Before you think about food stockpiles, generators, or barter items, you must anchor your wealth in something solid. In every financial crisis, the people who survive best are those who held assets that couldn't be erased with a keystroke or frozen by a bank. These are the foundations of financial resilience—the things you can count on when everything else turns to quicksand.

Precious Metals

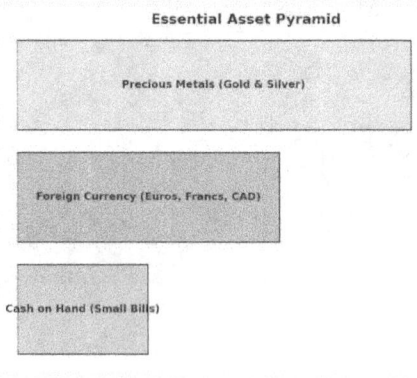

- **Gold and Silver** are not just shiny objects—they are time-tested money. For thousands of years, through empires rising and falling, these metals have held their value while paper currencies burned to nothing.

- **Practical Use:** Keep gold in small, divisible forms (coins, not just large bars) so it can be traded if needed. Silver, especially "junk silver" coins, is often more useful in daily barter.

- **The Key:** Precious metals are not about speculation —they're about preservation. Owning them ensures that part of your wealth is immune to inflation, defaults, or government manipulation.

Foreign Currency

- When the dollar falters, **strong foreign currencies** may provide breathing room. Euros, Swiss francs, and even Canadian dollars are often more stable and more easily trusted in a crisis.

- **How to Use Them:** Keep small stashes of these notes tucked away, just like cash. They can help if international trade shifts or if border economies remain functional while the U.S. dollar crumbles.

- **Reality Check:** You don't need to be an international banker—just a few hundred in foreign bills can make the difference between trade and desperation.

Cash on Hand

- Digital systems are fragile. A simple power outage or bank holiday makes debit cards, credit cards, and ATMs useless. **Physical cash becomes king—at least temporarily.**

- **Small Bills Matter:** Stock up on $1s, $5s, $10s, and $20s. In crisis, nobody wants to break a $100, and refusing it may be easier than giving change.

- **Emergency Edge:** Having cash in hand allows you to move fast—buying food, fuel, or medicine before panic clears the shelves.

✅ **Think:** *If the banks shut down tomorrow, what could I rely on to feed my family and keep us safe? Precious metals, foreign currency, and cash in small bills form the bedrock of your survival economy.*

STEP 2: BUILD TANGIBLE RESERVES

In a collapse, survival is about what you can hold in your hands, not what's sitting in a bank account. Tangible reserves are your **real-world safety net**—the supplies that keep your family alive and independent when outside systems fail.

Food: Stockpile **30–90 days' worth of shelf-stable foods**: rice, beans, oats, pasta, canned meats, canned vegetables, oils, and powdered milk.

- Include comfort foods like coffee, tea, and spices to maintain morale.

- Store in airtight containers or mylar bags with oxygen absorbers to extend shelf life.

Water: Rule of thumb: **1 gallon per person per day**. For a family of four, that's 120 gallons for a month.

- Use food-grade barrels, water bricks, or sealed bottles.

- Invest in **backup purification**: portable filters, purification tablets, or rainwater catchment systems.

Medicine: Stock up on **first-aid essentials**: bandages, antiseptics, pain relievers, and fever reducers.

• If possible, acquire **antibiotics** (consult a doctor or explore veterinary equivalents carefully).

• Don't forget hygiene items: soap, toothpaste, feminine products, and disinfectants. In a crisis, disease spreads fast.

Energy: Secure **multiple backup power sources**: solar panels, hand-crank chargers, and generators.

• Stock propane tanks, kerosene, or firewood depending on your location.

• Keep extra lighters, matches, and candles—cheap today, priceless tomorrow.

✅ **Ask Yourself:** Could my household function if the stores shut down for 60 days? If the answer is no, keep building.

STEP 3: SET UP EMERGENCY CASH FLOW

Even if the grid goes down or the dollar stumbles, life doesn't stop. Bills, barter, and unexpected costs will still arise—and without a steady flow of resources, your reserves will vanish faster than you expect. True resilience means creating **streams of value** that keep working, even in a crisis.

Key Strategies:

• 💵 **Hidden Stash**

Don't keep all your emergency cash in one spot. Divide it into multiple safe locations—such as a fireproof safe, hidden compartments, or even buried waterproof containers. That way, if one stash is discovered or stolen, you're not wiped out.

Tip: Keep part of it in small bills ($5s, $10s, $20s) for everyday trade.

• 🔧 **Side Income & Trade Skills**

Relying only on a job tied to fragile systems is dangerous. A small side hustle can become a lifeline. Think skills that remain useful no matter what: basic repairs, food preservation, tutoring, medical aid, or even creating barter goods like soap or firewood bundles. For those still online, freelance or digital work can provide cross-border payments in cryptocurrencies or foreign currency.

• 📄 **Debt Reduction**

High-interest credit cards and loans are like holes in your survival boat. Even in a stable system, they drag you down. In a crisis, creditors can still come after you—or worse, you could lose essential property. Paying off debt now is like buying freedom in advance.

✅ **Consider:** How can I create cash flow that survives even when the system doesn't? Whether it's a drawer of small bills, a trade you can fall back on, or a debt-free home, every step builds independence.

STEP 4: CREATE A FAMILY GO-BAG

Disasters almost never send a warning. Whether it's civil unrest, a sudden evacuation order, or a natural disaster, you may have only **minutes** to act. A pre-packed family go-bag ensures that you can leave immediately without scrambling for essentials—and without losing precious time.

What to Include:

- **Cash & Coins**

Carry small bills and coins—$1s, $5s, $10s, and quarters. In a breakdown, large bills may be impossible to spend. Cash buys food, fuel, or shelter when cards and ATMs are down.

- **Important Documents**

Make waterproof copies (or keep digital encrypted versions on a USB drive):

- IDs and passports
- Property deeds and insurance papers
- Medical records, prescriptions, and vaccination cards
- Emergency contacts and family plan details

- **Emergency Supplies**

- Flashlight and spare batteries
- Portable first-aid kit
- Maps (paper, not digital) and a compass
- Water filter or purification tablets
- Multi-tool or knife

- **Personal & Family Items**

- Prescription medications
- Glasses or contacts
- Baby diapers, formula, wipes
- Comfort items—like a small blanket, toy, or even chocolate—to ease stress for children

✅ **Rule to Remember:** If you had only **10 minutes** to leave your house, this bag should carry your lifeline. Pack light, but pack smart. Keep the bag in an easy-to-grab location—near the front door, in a car trunk, or by your emergency exit. Check it every 6 months to refresh food, water, and medical supplies.

PART IV – THE FAMILY EMERGENCY PLAN

When disaster strikes, the difference between chaos and survival often comes down to one thing: preparation. A family without a plan risks confusion, fear, and dangerous mistakes. A family with a plan moves with confidence, knowing who does what, where to go, and how to stay connected.

This section provides you with the framework to build a **practical, step-by-step emergency plan** tailored to your household. From evacuation routes to communication strategies, from securing documents to preparing a go-bag, every detail matters.

Remember: survival is not just about stockpiles and supplies—it's about **coordination, clarity, and unity**. When each member of your family knows their role, your household becomes a resilient team, ready to face the unexpected.

CHAPTER 9
PREPARING YOUR HOUSEHOLD

WHEN CRISIS LOOMS, the first line of defense is not a stockpile of supplies—it's your household's ability to work as a unit. Preparedness begins at home, and the stronger your family's foundation, the better your chances of navigating turmoil with resilience and calm.

EXPLAINING THE CRISIS TO YOUR KIDS WITHOUT CAUSING PANIC

Children are natural observers. They notice changes in tone, worried looks, whispered conversations, and even small disruptions to routine. If you don't explain what's happening, they will fill in the gaps with their own imagination—which often creates more fear than the reality itself. The key is balance: **honesty without alarm, empowerment without overwhelming them.**

- **Be Honest, Not Alarming**

Kids deserve the truth, but filtered through age-appropriate language. Instead of saying, *"The world is collapsing,"* you might explain:

"Sometimes power or money systems don't work the way they should. That's why we practice being ready—like how we do fire drills at school."

By framing it as preparation rather than doom, children learn to see resilience as normal.

- **Empower, Don't Frighten**

Children feel safer when they have something useful to do. Assign them small, meaningful roles—like checking if flashlights have batteries, helping pack snacks for the go-bag, or keeping track of their own favorite blanket or toy. These tasks aren't just busywork: they teach responsibility, reduce fear, and remind kids that they are part of the solution, not passive bystanders.

- **Create Reassurance**

Fear thrives in uncertainty. Regularly remind your children that your family has a plan, and that no matter what happens, you will face it together. Reinforce routines where possible—family meals, bedtime stories, or even prayer—because consistency anchors children emotionally during uncertainty.

☑ **Rule:** Kids who understand the plan are calmer and more cooperative during emergencies. By giving them clarity and responsibility, you transform panic into trust and fear into resilience.

ASSIGNING ROLES AND RESPONSIBILITIES

In moments of crisis, panic and confusion can waste valuable time. The best way to avoid this is to establish clear roles for each family member *before* an emergency ever happens. When everyone knows their duty, the household functions like a well-trained team.

- **Parents**: Take charge of the big picture—major decisions, safeguarding finances, and ensuring security measures are in place. They act as the anchor when everyone else looks for direction.

- **Teenagers**: Strong enough to carry supplies and mature enough to follow instructions, teens can be a huge asset. They can help with setting up camp, watching younger siblings, handling radios or phones, and even managing a barter exchange.

- **Children**: Younger kids thrive when they're given simple, meaningful roles. Tasks like carrying their own small "comfort bag," feeding pets, or helping check flashlight batteries give them a sense of purpose and control.

- **Backup Roles**: Life is unpredictable. If the parent responsible for finances is unavailable, another family member should know how to access cash, documents, or supplies. Every role should have at least one backup.

☑ **Think of your household as a survival team.** Every member matters. Clear responsibilities ensure that no one is left guessing and that critical needs are met quickly and calmly.

STORING AND SECURING CRITICAL DOCUMENTS AND IDS

In a true emergency, your documents can be as vital as food or water. They are the keys that unlock access to aid, allow you to cross borders, reclaim property, and prove who you are when systems are strained or broken. Losing them during chaos can set your recovery back weeks—or even make survival harder.

What to Store:

- **Identity Documents:** Birth certificates, passports, driver's licenses, Social Security cards, and state IDs.

- **Property & Financial Records:** Home deeds, car titles, loan papers, insurance policies, bank account details.

- **Medical Records:** Vaccination history, prescriptions, allergies, and key medical conditions.

- **Emergency Extras:** Marriage certificates, wills, and any power-of-attorney or guardianship papers.

Where to Store:

- **Primary Storage:** Originals locked in a waterproof, fireproof safe at home. Choose one that is both hidden and bolted down.

- **Secondary Storage:** Copies stored in your **family go-bag** in waterproof sleeves.

- **Digital Backups:** An encrypted USB drive with scans of all documents, plus a secure cloud backup if internet access remains available. This ensures that even if paper copies are lost, digital versions can be retrieved later.

Quick Access:

In an evacuation, you may have less than 10 minutes to leave. All critical papers must be stored so they can be grabbed in seconds—not scattered across drawers and cabinets.

☑️ *Rule: In a crisis, your documents are your passport to recovery—guard them like treasure.*

CHAPTER 10
COMMUNICATION WHEN SYSTEMS FAIL

WHEN CRISES STRIKE, one of the first systems to collapse is communication. Cell towers may go dark, the internet may crash, and phone lines may jam. Yet, staying connected with your family, neighbors, and community is essential for safety and coordination. A strong communication plan ensures that even if modern systems fail, you won't be left in silence.

HOW TO STAY CONNECTED WITHOUT INTERNET OR CELL TOWERS

When digital systems fail, communication must return to its most practical and resilient forms. Being cut off from your family or community can be just as dangerous as running out of food or water. That's why investing in multiple communication methods is essential.

- **Walkie-Talkies (FRS/GMRS Radios):**

These small, handheld radios are one of the easiest tools for emergency communication. Affordable and simple to use, they can operate on common frequencies with a range of one to five miles depending on terrain. Perfect for keeping in touch within a neighborhood, on a small farm, or during evacuation travel. Always keep spare batteries, or better yet, rechargeable ones with a solar charger.

- **Two-Way Radios (HAM/Amateur Radio):**

HAM radios have been the backbone of emergency communication for decades. Their range extends far beyond walkie-talkies—sometimes across states or even countries when conditions allow. They do require a license to use legally in normal times, but learning the basics now could be a lifesaver later.

In collapse scenarios, regulations may no longer apply, and these radios could connect you to wider networks of survivors.

- **Signal Systems:**

Technology is powerful, but simple tools should never be underestimated. Whistles can signal distress or location, mirrors can flash signals over long distances in daylight, and pre-arranged knocks, gestures, or coded phrases can help families communicate silently and securely. These methods don't require power, bandwidth, or devices—just planning and practice.

☑ **Rule:** Never rely on a single method of communication. Redundancy is survival. The family that has radios, signal systems, and rally points will always stay a step ahead of the family that depends only on cell service.

SETTING FAMILY RALLY POINTS AND FALLBACK LOCATIONS

In an emergency, confusion is as dangerous as the crisis itself. Power outages, civil unrest, or sudden evacuations can scatter family members. Without a working phone or internet, how will you regroup? The answer is simple: **pre-planned rally points.**

- **Primary Rally Point (Home Zone):** Choose a safe and obvious spot within sight of your home. It could be the backyard, a large tree, or even a trusted neighbor's porch. This is the first place everyone should head to if separated inside or near the house.

- **Secondary Rally Point (Community Zone):** Select a spot a short walk or drive away, ideally within 1–5 miles. Parks, churches, or the home of a reliable friend or relative are excellent options. This covers situations where your neighborhood is compromised or unsafe.

- **Fallback Location (Escape Zone):** Finally, establish a distant safe house or rural retreat, possibly owned by family or trusted friends. This is your evacuation site if staying in the city or town becomes impossible.

☑ **The Key:** Practice these routes as a family. Every member—even children—should know them by memory, just like they would a home fire drill. A clear plan eliminates hesitation and panic when seconds matter most.

RADIO, WALKIE-TALKIES, AND ANALOG BACKUPS

When the grid goes dark and cell towers fall silent, communication tools that most people overlook become lifelines. Radios, walkie-talkies, and even old-fashioned analog methods give families and communities a way to share information and coordinate survival.

Battery Life & Power Planning

Radios and walkie-talkies are only as reliable as their power supply. Stockpile extra AA and AAA batteries, and invest in rechargeable ones paired with a small solar charger. This ensures your devices won't become useless after a week. Keep batteries stored in a cool, dry place to extend shelf life. In long-term emergencies, the ability to generate your own power—whether through solar panels, hand cranks, or car adapters—will make your radios last indefinitely.

Emergency Radios for Critical Updates

A solar-powered or hand-crank AM/FM/NOAA weather radio is one of the smartest investments you can make. Unlike cell phones, these radios don't rely on towers or internet connections. Government agencies, local municipalities, and emergency broadcasters use radio frequencies to share evacuation notices, weather alerts, and security updates. Having one in your home and another in your go-bag keeps you connected to the outside world when others are blind.

Walkie-Talkies for Local Coordination

Family Radio Service (FRS) and General Mobile Radio Service (GMRS) walkie-talkies allow short-range communication—perfect for keeping in touch with family members spread across a neighborhood, farm, or small town. They're inexpensive, easy to use, and don't require complex setup. A few simple call signs and pre-arranged check-in times prevent chaos and confusion.

HAM Radios for Wider Reach

Amateur (HAM) radios require a license to operate legally under normal conditions, but in a true collapse, they become invaluable. HAM operators can communicate across states or even internationally, bypassing the broken internet and connecting survivors with crucial information. If possible, take the time to get licensed now and learn the basics—it's a skill that could save lives.

Analog Backups for Human Networks

Technology can still fail, even at the small scale. That's where analog methods shine. Pen and paper notes on bulletin boards, chalk markings at designated community spots, or even signals like tied ribbons, stones, or lantern lights can communicate essential information when devices fail. A message board at a local church, school, or town hall can become the heartbeat of a neighborhood.

Digital networks may vanish overnight, but human networks—strengthened by preparation—remain.

CHAPTER 11
THE FAMILY ACTION MANUAL

PREPARATION IS MORE than just supplies—it's about having a clear, practiced plan that your family can follow under stress. This chapter provides templates, tools, and drills to ensure your household is not just stocked, but ready.

CUSTOMIZABLE EMERGENCY PLAN TEMPLATES

Every household has different needs, which is why a "one-size-fits-all" emergency plan doesn't exist. A written, customized plan gives structure during chaos and ensures no critical step is overlooked. The goal is simple: every member of your family should know where to go, who to contact, and what to do—even if you aren't there to guide them.

What to Include:

- **Emergency Contacts:**

Write down names, phone numbers, and addresses for local friends, relatives, and at least one out-of-town contact. In large-scale disasters, local lines may be jammed, but long-distance calls sometimes go through. Out-of-town relatives can serve as a central hub to relay information between separated family members.

- **Meeting Points:**

Define three levels of rally locations:

  - **Primary:** A spot right outside your home (like a backyard oak tree) if you need to exit quickly.

- **Secondary:** A location in your neighborhood (like a church, park, or trusted neighbor's house) in case home isn't safe.

- **Fallback:** A distant location (relative's home, rural retreat) if evacuation becomes unavoidable.

• **Escape Routes:**

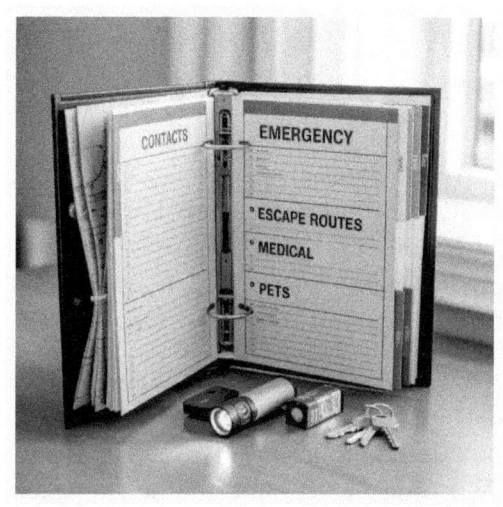

Draw a simple floor plan of your home and mark at least two exits from every room. Teach kids how to open windows safely or locate fire ladders if needed. For neighborhood escape, highlight multiple routes in case one is blocked by traffic, fire, or unrest.

• **Medical Needs:**

Record all allergies, critical prescriptions, and chronic conditions for each family member. Designate who carries medicines and keep extras in your go-bag. In stressful situations, small details (like a child's asthma inhaler or a parent's blood pressure pills) can mean the difference between safety and danger.

• **Pet Plan:**

Pets are family too. Prepare a section for food rations, water, carriers, and veterinary documents. If you must evacuate, many shelters only accept animals with proof of vaccines. Planning ahead prevents heartbreaking choices later.

✅ **Tip:** Print at least two copies—one for your go-bag and one for a central home location (such as a kitchen cabinet or family binder). For extra security, keep a digital version on an encrypted USB or password-protected cloud drive.

HOUSEHOLD SURVIVAL KIT: WHAT EVERY FAMILY SHOULD HAVE

A true emergency kit goes beyond a few flashlights and bottled water. It is the backbone of your household's resilience when modern systems fail. The goal is simple: if your family couldn't leave home for two weeks, your kit should cover every essential need—water, food, health, light, and communication.

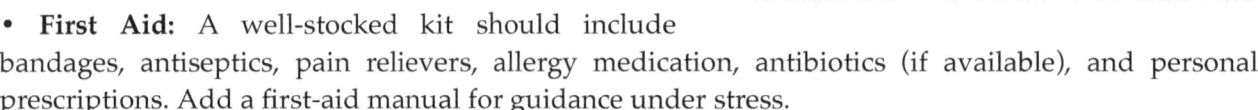

- **Water:** Store at least one gallon per person per day for drinking and hygiene. For a family of four, that's 28 gallons for a week. Supplement with water filters, purification tablets, and a collapsible container for collecting rainwater.

- **Food:** Choose non-perishable staples—rice, beans, oats, canned meats, canned vegetables, peanut butter, powdered milk. Don't forget a manual can opener. Pack food in airtight containers to extend shelf life.

- **First Aid:** A well-stocked kit should include bandages, antiseptics, pain relievers, allergy medication, antibiotics (if available), and personal prescriptions. Add a first-aid manual for guidance under stress.

- **Light & Power:** Headlamps, lanterns, and flashlights with extra batteries keep you mobile at night. Solar chargers or hand-crank generators ensure your devices can recharge without the grid.

- **Communication:** Walkie-talkies or FRS/GMRS radios let you stay in touch nearby. An emergency AM/FM or shortwave radio helps you hear government updates and weather alerts. Keep a backup power bank charged and stored.

- **Tools:** Include a multipurpose knife, duct tape, paracord, matches or lighters, and fire starters. A small toolkit (screwdriver, wrench, pliers) is invaluable for quick repairs.

- **Hygiene:** Stock soap, hand sanitizer, feminine products, toothbrushes, sanitation wipes, trash bags, and even a small camping toilet if possible. Cleanliness prevents illness.

- **Documents & Cash:** Store waterproof copies of IDs, deeds, insurance papers, medical records, and a modest stash of small bills. Keep everything in a fireproof pouch or folder.

✅ **Rule of Thumb:** If you couldn't leave home for 14 days, your survival kit should allow your family to eat, drink, stay clean, stay warm, communicate, and protect important records without external help.

PRACTICE DRILLS: TESTING YOUR FAMILY'S READINESS

Practice Drills: Testing Your Family's Readiness

Knowledge without practice fades quickly. A written plan is only as strong as your family's ability to carry it out under stress. Regular drills transform theory into habit, making preparedness second nature.

- **Blackout Drill:** Once a month, simulate a power outage by cutting the breakers for an evening. Practice cooking with alternative methods, lighting the home with lanterns or flashlights, and communicating without phones or Wi-Fi. Kids will quickly learn that candles and radios replace lightbulbs and screens.

- **Evacuation Drill:** Time how long it takes to grab your go-bags, secure critical documents, load the car, and leave. Choose a rally point and test whether everyone arrives safely. Track the time—it should get faster with each attempt.

- **Medical Drill:** Walk through simple first aid scenarios: cleaning a wound, using a bandage, or locating prescription medications. Even young children can be shown where the first aid kit is kept and how to call for help if needed.

- **Role Rotation:** Allow kids and teens to temporarily take on adult responsibilities (with supervision). A teenager can practice operating the radio, while younger kids can rehearse gathering their comfort items. This builds both competence and confidence.

✅ *Lesson: In a real crisis, panic slows people down. Drills transform panic into action. By rehearsing in advance, your family will respond calmly, quickly, and effectively when it matters most.*

PART V – THRIVING AFTER THE COLLAPSE

Survival is not just about enduring the darkest days—it's about **rebuilding a stable, secure, and meaningful life** once the storm has passed.

In this part, we focus on how to transform collapse into an opportunity for renewal.

When economic and social systems fall apart, returning to stability requires creativity, resilience, and community spirit. Stockpiles alone won't be enough—you must know how to grow, build, and cooperate. Here we will explore how to:

• **Cultivate a sustainable local economy** through bartering, family gardens, and new forms of work.

• **Create resilient communities** that can protect, trade, and thrive together.

• **Build lasting independence** with renewable energy, practical knowledge, and strong social bonds.

• **Find meaning and hope** in a simpler way of life, where value is measured not in dollars but in skills, relationships, and faith.

This section is not only about survival—it's about **thriving**: turning crisis into a return to roots, where families and communities emerge stronger than they were before collapse.

CHAPTER 12
REBUILDING IN THE NEW ECONOMY

TURNING CRISIS INTO OPPORTUNITY: BUSINESSES THAT THRIVE POST-COLLAPSE

HISTORY IS full of examples showing that even when governments collapse or currencies lose their value, **commerce never disappears**—it merely transforms. People will always need food, water, medicine, warmth, and tools to survive. After the fall of the dollar, the businesses that thrive won't be Silicon Valley tech firms or Wall Street hedge funds—they will be the humble but powerful services that keep life going.

- **Food Production & Preservation**

In a world where grocery stores are unreliable, food becomes the new gold. Families who can grow vegetables, raise chickens or rabbits, and preserve their harvest through canning, pickling, drying, or smoking suddenly hold incredible power. A few extra jars of preserved beans or a steady supply of eggs can be traded for fuel, medicine, or labor. What was once a hobby garden can quickly turn into a lifeline for neighbors and a source of income in the new economy.

- **Repair & Maintenance**

When global supply chains grind to a halt, every tool, machine, and piece of equipment becomes irreplaceable. A simple water pump, bicycle, or solar panel could mean the difference between survival and collapse. Those with mechanical skills—able to repair engines, sharpen knives, mend clothing, or maintain energy systems—instantly transform from ordinary workers into essential community members. In a collapsed economy, the handyman, blacksmith, or tinkerer is more valuable than a stockbroker.

- **Health & Medicine**

Hospitals and pharmacies may close or run out of supplies, leaving entire communities without medical care. In such times, those with even **basic medical training** or knowledge of herbal remedies become guardians of life. Antibiotics, bandages, painkillers, and hygiene items turn into priceless assets. A person who can treat wounds, manage infections, or guide others in safe natural alternatives doesn't just provide a service—they provide hope.

- **Energy & Heat**

When the grid goes dark, the ability to create light, warmth, and power becomes the new measure of wealth. Businesses and households that can cut firewood, install small solar setups, maintain generators, or store fuel become vital to community survival. Imagine trading a bag of firewood for a week's worth of food, or exchanging the use of a solar panel for medical care. Energy is freedom—and those who can provide it will never go hungry.

- **Barter Trade & Logistics**

In every collapsed economy, barter markets spring up. Farmers bring eggs, mechanics bring tools, and families bring surplus supplies to exchange. But just as important as the goods themselves are the **organizers**—the people who manage fair trades, set up small markets, and create systems of trust. In chaos, reliable middlemen become indispensable. Those who can **connect people with what they need**—transporting, trading, or negotiating—become the backbone of the new economy.

Crisis destroys many businesses—but it also opens new doors. The collapse of one system is simply the birth of another. Those who can adapt, provide essentials, and solve real human needs will not only survive but thrive.

✅ **The truth:** Collapse doesn't end trade—it changes it. The new "entrepreneurs" are growers, fixers, healers, energy providers, and barter leaders.

FROM SURVIVAL TO SELF-RELIANCE

The first months after collapse are focused on the basics—food, water, warmth, and safety. These are the days of rationing supplies and relying on stockpiles. But stockpiles run out. Cans get eaten, batteries die, and stored water eventually runs low. That's why true resilience demands a shift in mindset: from simply *surviving* day to day, to becoming truly *self-reliant*.

Self-reliance is not about isolation—it's about breaking free from fragile systems and creating sustainable independence.

• **Grow Instead of Buy:** A garden isn't just a hobby anymore—it's your lifeline. Learning how to grow vegetables, plant fruit trees, raise chickens, or even manage a few goats transforms your family from consumers into producers. Seed saving ensures your food supply renews year after year.

• **Produce Instead of Consume:** Post-collapse, every household skill becomes an economic advantage. Soap making, sewing clothes, repairing shoes, or crafting tools reduce reliance on broken supply chains and give you goods to trade.

• **Teach & Share Knowledge:** In a fractured society, knowledge becomes a new form of currency. The person who can teach others to grow food, build a shelter, or preserve meat becomes indispensable. Sharing knowledge not only helps others—it builds alliances and influence.

• **Strengthen Community Roots:** While one self-reliant family can survive, a self-reliant community can *thrive*. Imagine a neighborhood where one family grows food, another raises livestock, another repairs tools, and another provides medical knowledge. Together, they create resilience that no single household could achieve alone.

✅ *The lesson: After collapse, wealth will not be measured in dollars or stocks—it will be measured in **food security, practical skills, and trust between people**. The journey from survival to self-reliance is not just about staying alive—it's about laying the foundation for a new, sustainable way of living.*

CHAPTER 13
BUILDING A RESILIENT MINDSET

SURVIVAL IS NEVER JUST about food, water, or supplies—it begins in the mind. In times of collapse, fear spreads faster than hunger, and despair destroys communities faster than violence. A resilient mindset is the foundation that transforms preparation into strength. It is what allows a family not just to endure the storm, but to come out stronger on the other side.

MANAGING FEAR AND UNCERTAINTY

Fear is natural, but unchecked it paralyzes. In survival situations, fear can be as dangerous as hunger or cold—it clouds judgment, fuels rash decisions, and spreads quickly within a family or community. The goal is not to eliminate fear, but to master it and transform it into alertness and focus.

- **Control What You Can:** Fear grows when everything feels out of control. Break survival into manageable steps. Did you secure clean water today? Did you prepare a hot meal? Did you check your supplies? Each small victory is proof that you *can* act, that progress is being made, and that you are not helpless.

- **Limit Panic Triggers:** Chaos often brings a flood of rumors, speculation, and worst-case scenarios. Consuming constant doom-talk—whether from neighbors, social media, or the radio—can magnify panic. Establish limits: check for updates at set times, but don't dwell. Instead, maintain daily rituals—mealtimes, chores, even family games—that anchor life in a sense of order and normalcy.

- **Faith & Perspective:** History shows us that the strongest survivors aren't always the strongest physically, but those who have an inner anchor. Whether through faith in God, personal philosophy, or the belief that you are protecting future generations, having a higher purpose gives meaning to struggle. Fear loses its grip when replaced by conviction.

☑ **Rule:** Fear thrives in the unknown. Replace fear with knowledge and preparation. Each skill learned, each plan rehearsed, each resource secured pushes fear aside and strengthens confidence.

TEACHING YOUR FAMILY CONFIDENCE AND ADAPTABILITY

In uncertain times, the most valuable inheritance you can give your family is not food or money, but the mindset to face adversity with calm strength. Confidence and adaptability are learned behaviors—and the family unit is the training ground.

• **Confidence Through Practice:** Just like fire drills in school, repeating survival routines at home—such as cooking on a camp stove, tending a small garden, or using walkie-talkies—turns abstract "plans" into muscle memory. When challenges arise, your family won't freeze; they'll act, because they've practiced it before.

• **Celebrate Small Wins:** Building confidence isn't about perfection, it's about progress. Every successful drill, every meal cooked from stored food, every garden harvest is a victory. Mark these milestones—celebrate them at the dinner table or keep a family "prep journal." Each achievement strengthens resilience and bonds your household.

• **Flexibility Over Rigidity:** In collapse scenarios, rigid thinking breaks under pressure. A backup plan for water, an alternate rally point, or simply the willingness to try a new method keeps morale high and options open. Teach your family that shifting course isn't failure—it's smart survival.

☑ **Lesson:** True survival is not about memorizing a single plan—it's about cultivating a spirit of adaptability. Those who can stay calm, flexible, and confident in the face of change will not only endure but grow stronger together.

THE LONG VIEW: PREPARING NOT JUST TO SURVIVE, BUT TO PROSPER

Survival is only the first chapter in the story of collapse. True resilience comes from looking beyond the present struggle and imagining a future where you and your community do more than just endure—you build, adapt, and prosper. Survival buys time; vision creates legacy.

• **Think Beyond Stockpiles:** Stored food and water carry you through the early days, but they eventually run out. Seeds, tools, and the skills to use them become the foundation of ongoing stability. Unlike canned goods, knowledge and skill never expire.

• **Build Traditions of Strength:** Shared rituals—whether family meals, evening prayer, or community workdays—keep morale high and give meaning to hardship. These small traditions transform survival into culture, keeping families and communities rooted.

- **Plant for Tomorrow:** Every choice should be an investment in the future. Planting fruit trees, mentoring children in self-sufficiency, or building strong ties with neighbors all pay dividends that grow with time. In survival, as in life, those who think long-term become the leaders others depend on.

- **Measure Wealth Differently:** Post-collapse prosperity is not measured in dollars or possessions, but in security, relationships, and the ability to regenerate resources. A family that can feed itself, trade fairly, and pass on wisdom is wealthy in the truest sense.

✅ **Truth:** The resilient mindset does not see crisis as an ending. It sees it as soil—fertile ground in which new life, stronger traditions, and a lasting legacy can grow.

CONCLUSION

RECAP OF THE MOST URGENT STEPS TO TAKE TODAY

Preparedness is not about living in fear—it's about taking responsibility for the people who count on you. The good news is that the most powerful steps are also the most practical:

- **Food & Water Reserves:** Start with a 30–90 day supply of non-perishable food and clean drinking water. This is the foundation of survival. When shelves are empty, your family will eat because you planned ahead. Add water filters and purification tablets to extend your supply.

- **Critical Documents:** Birth certificates, IDs, deeds, medical records, and insurance papers are just as valuable as food. Secure them in a waterproof, fireproof safe, keep copies in your go-bag, and back them up digitally. Without these, recovery after crisis becomes an uphill battle.

- **Family Go-Bag:** Emergencies rarely give warnings. A ready-to-grab bag with cash, documents, first aid, and personal essentials means you can evacuate in minutes without losing what matters most.

- **Communication Plan:** Don't assume phones will work. Establish rally points, backup meeting spots, and analog communication methods like radios or walkie-talkies. Confusion kills—clarity saves lives.

- **Home Security:** Think in layers—lights, locks, reinforced doors, and safe rooms. Make your home a hard target so that threats pass you by. Remember: prevention is better than confrontation.

- **Financial Strength:** Pay down crippling debt before it traps you during crisis. Diversify your assets—cash in small bills, some precious metals, and essentials like food, medicine, and tools. These hold value when systems fail.

- **Skills Over Stuff:** Supplies can run out, but skills compound over time. Learn to grow food, preserve it, repair tools, and administer first aid. In a barter economy, what you can *do* will matter more than what you *have*.

☑ **Act Now:** Preparation loses its power if delayed. A half-filled pantry today is worth more than an empty promise to prepare tomorrow. Every small step compounds into resilience. Delay is the real enemy—take action while you still can.

THE MINDSET SHIFT: FROM VICTIM TO LEADER

In times of chaos, people fall into two groups: those who freeze, waiting for someone else to save them, and those who rise to the moment. The difference is not strength, wealth, or luck—it is **mindset.**

If you see yourself as a victim of events, every setback will feel crushing. You'll wait for help that may never come, and you'll live at the mercy of others. But if you embrace your role as protector, provider, and leader, everything changes. A leader doesn't wait for permission—he or she takes action, however small, to secure stability for loved ones.

True leadership in crisis is not about having all the answers. It's about:

• **Calm in the Storm:** Panic spreads like fire. A steady tone of voice, clear instructions, and composed actions reassure others that survival is possible.

• **Decisions Under Pressure:** Perfect choices may be impossible, but timely decisions save lives. Leaders accept responsibility and move forward instead of hesitating.

• **Service Over Self:** Leadership is rooted in sacrifice—placing the needs of your family and community above your own comfort.

• **Creating Hope:** When others only see fear and scarcity, a leader points to solutions, opportunities, and the possibility of rebuilding stronger than before.

☑ **Lesson:** Leadership is not about titles—it's about presence. By shifting from victim to leader, you become the anchor your family and community need. In uncertain times, your mindset is as valuable as food or water, because it determines whether you merely survive—or inspire others to thrive.

A CALL TO ACTION

The future may hold uncertainty, but your choices today do not. You have the power, right now, to decide whether your family faces crisis with fear—or with confidence.

Start with the basics: **secure your home, build your reserves, practice your drills, and strengthen your family's resilience.** These are not complicated tasks; they are simple, deliberate steps that multiply your chances of survival and peace of mind. Don't wait for the next headline, the next blackout, or the next siren to signal danger. By then, it will already be too late.

Preparedness is not paranoia—it is responsibility. Every gallon of water stored, every plan rehearsed, every neighbor you connect with moves you one step closer to safety and strength. More than that, it shifts your family from being vulnerable dependents to being anchors of stability when others are adrift.

This is your moment to transform fear into readiness, uncertainty into action, and crisis into opportunity. When systems collapse, **leaders emerge**—and your family needs you to be that leader.

The collapse of systems does not mean the collapse of life. With preparation, courage, and faith, you will not only endure—you will thrive. You will become the rock that others lean on, guiding your loved ones and your community into a stronger, more resilient tomorrow.

BONUS MATERIALS: ALL BONUS MATERIALS CAN BE DOWNLOADED BY SCANNING THE QR CODE BELOW.

All bonus materials can be downloaded by scanning the QR Code below.

APPENDIX A – EMERGENCY FAMILY SURVIVAL PLAN

This plan is designed to be simple, direct, and ready-to-use. Fill it out with your family today, print extra copies, and keep one in your go-bag, one at home, and one with a trusted contact.

1. Emergency Contacts

- Local Family & Friends: _____
- Out-of-Town Contact: _____
- Doctor / Medical Contact: _____
- School / Workplace Contact: _____

2. Meeting Points

- **Primary (near home):** _____
- **Secondary (within a few miles):** _____
- **Fallback (long-distance safe location):** _____

3. Escape Routes

- **From House (fire/emergency):** _____
- **From Neighborhood (larger evacuation):** _____

4. Medical Needs

- Allergies: _____
- Prescriptions: _____
- Responsible Person: _____

5. Pet Plan

- Food & Supplies Location: _____
- Carrier/Leash Location: _____
- Veterinary Contact: _____

☑ **Tip:** Review and update this plan **every 6 months** or whenever your family situation changes.

📌 **Downloadable PDF:** Scan the QR code at the end of this book to access a printable, customizable version of this plan.

APPENDIX B – FINANCIAL COLLAPSE CHECKLIST

Use this one-page reference to stay focused when stress is high. Print it. Post it. Practice it.

✅ **Step 1: Secure Essential Assets**

- Gold / Silver Coins stored safely
- Small stash of foreign currency
- Cash on hand (small bills, hidden in multiple spots)

✅ **Step 2: Build Tangible Reserves**

- Food (30–90 days: rice, beans, canned goods, oils)
- Water (1 gallon per person/day + filters, tablets)
- Medicine (first aid kit, prescriptions, hygiene supplies)
- Energy (firewood, propane, generator, solar backup)

✅ **Step 3: Set Up Emergency Cash Flow**

- Hidden cash stash split into safe places
- Side income or barter skill identified
- High-interest debts reduced or eliminated

✅ **Step 4: Family Go-Bag Ready**

- Cash & coins in small bills
- IDs, deeds, insurance, medical documents

- Flashlight, batteries, first aid kit, maps, water filter
- Personal items (prescriptions, baby needs, comfort items)

📌 **Quick Rule:** If the banks closed tomorrow, could your family function for 60 days without outside help?

📌 **Downloadable PDF:** Scan the QR code at the end of this book for a printable checklist to keep in your kitchen, safe, or binder.

APPENDIX C – EXCEL TRACKER (BUDGET & INVENTORY SHEET)

Why use it?

In a crisis, memory fails. Supplies vanish faster than expected, and overspending can drain cash reserves. An Excel tracker keeps your prepping clear, organized, and under control.

What the Excel Tracker Includes

1 Budget Overview

- Columns for **Category** (Food, Water, Medicine, Energy, Tools, Miscellaneous).
- Planned budget vs. actual spending.
- Automatic totals to see if you are overspending.

2 Inventory Sheet

- Columns for **Item**, **Quantity on Hand**, **Target Quantity**, **Expiration Date**, and **Location Stored**.
- Color-coded alerts for items expiring soon.
- Easy way to track rotations (first in, first out).

3 Reorder & Restock List

- Separate tab that pulls items below target level.
- Quick reference for shopping or bartering.

4 Cash & Assets Log

- Track where cash is hidden (without exact addresses, just "Safe #1" / "Envelope A").
- Precious metals, foreign currency, and barter items listed with current values.

🛠 How to Use It

- **Update Weekly:** Add what you've bought, remove what you've used.
- **Highlight Priorities:** Mark items running low in red.
- **Plan Ahead:** Note expiration dates and set reminders for rotation.
- **Share Access:** Save a copy on an encrypted USB; print a hard copy for the family binder.

✅ **Result:** With this tracker, you'll know exactly what you have, what you need, and how long your household can last—no guessing, no waste, no panic.

📌 **Downloadable File:** Scan the QR code at the end of this book to download your ready-to-use Excel sheet.

APPENDIX D – EMERGENCY FAMILY SURVIVAL PLAN (PRINTABLE TEMPLATE)

Why it matters:

In the chaos of a real emergency, your family won't have time to debate or search for answers. A written plan ensures clarity, unity, and speed. This template is designed to be **filled out by hand** and kept both digitally (PDF/USB) and physically (printed, inside your go-bag and on a kitchen wall).

Customizable Sections

1 Emergency Contacts

- Local Friends/Neighbors: _____

- Out-of-Town Contact: _____

- Doctor/Clinic: _____

- Emergency Services: _____

2 Meeting Points

- Primary (near home): _____

- Secondary (in town): _____

- Fallback (out of town/rural): _____

3 Escape Routes

- From House (fire or immediate threat): _____

- From Neighborhood (evacuation): _____

- Pre-checked alternate routes: _____

4 Roles & Responsibilities

- Parent/Guardian 1: _____
- Parent/Guardian 2: _____
- Teenagers: _____
- Children: _____
- Backup Role Assignments: _____

5 Medical Needs

- Allergies: _____
- Prescriptions: _____
- Responsible Person: _____

6 Pet Plan

- Food & Water Needs: _____
- Carrier/Leash Location: _____
- Veterinary Records: _____

7 Go-Bag Checklist Confirmation

- Cash: ☐
- IDs & Documents: ☐
- First Aid Kit: ☐
- Flashlight & Batteries: ☐
- Water & Snacks: ☐
- Prescriptions: ☐
- Comfort Items for Kids: ☐

📌 **How to Use the Template**

- **Print Multiple Copies:** One in the home binder, one in the go-bag, and one given to a trusted relative or neighbor.

- **Update Quarterly:** Review contacts, prescriptions, and rally points every 3 months.

- **Practice It:** Run through the plan as a drill—make sure every family member knows what to do.

✅ **Result:** With this template, your family has a clear, written roadmap that eliminates hesitation and confusion when seconds matter.

📌 **Downloadable PDF:** Scan the QR code at the end of this book to get your printable version of the Family Survival Plan.

APPENDIX E – FINANCIAL COLLAPSE CHECKLIST (ONE-PAGE QUICK REFERENCE)

Purpose:

When the financial system falters, clarity and speed are critical. This **one-page checklist** keeps you focused on the actions that matter most—no panic, just execution.

✅ Step 1: Secure Essential Assets

- ☐ Gold and silver coins (small denominations)
- ☐ Small stashes of foreign currency (euros, francs, Canadian dollars)
- ☐ Cash in small bills (hidden in multiple safe spots)

✅ Step 2: Build Tangible Reserves

- ☐ Food (30–90 days: rice, beans, canned goods, oils)
- ☐ Water (1 gallon per person per day + filters)
- ☐ Medicine (antibiotics, pain relievers, prescriptions, hygiene)
- ☐ Energy (firewood, propane, generator fuel, solar panels)

✅ Step 3: Set Up Emergency Cash Flow

- ☐ Hidden emergency cash split into safe locations
- ☐ Side income or barter skill identified (repair, food, services)
- ☐ High-interest debt reduced/eliminated

✅ Step 4: Family Go-Bag (Financial Focus)

- ☐ Cash & coins (small bills)

- ☐ Critical documents (IDs, deeds, insurance, medical)
- ☐ Digital backups (encrypted USB or secure cloud)

✅ Step 5: Protection & Security

- ☐ Fireproof, waterproof safe for originals
- ☐ Multiple layers of home security (locks, lighting, safe storage)
- ☐ Family roles assigned for asset protection

📌 How to Use This Checklist

- Print it. Keep it in your family binder and go-bag.
- Review monthly. Update reserves, cash, and documents.
- Train your family. Everyone should know where cash, food, and documents are located.

⚡ Final Reminder:

Wealth after collapse is measured in food, water, medicine, energy, and skills—not in digital numbers. This checklist ensures you always have the essentials covered.

📌 **Downloadable PDF:** Scan the QR code at the end of this book to print your **Financial Collapse Quick Reference**.

APPENDIX F – EXCEL TRACKER (BUDGET & INVENTORY SHEET FOR PREPPING SUPPLIES)

Keeping track of what you own—and what you still need—is the backbone of smart preparedness. This **Excel sheet** is a living document that helps you manage your resources, spot shortages, and plan purchases without guesswork.

What's Inside the Excel Tracker

1. Budget Planner (Monthly & Annual)

- Columns for **income, essential expenses, and prepping expenses**
- Automatic calculation of how much can be safely allocated to supplies
- Color-coded alerts when overspending occurs

2. Food Inventory Table

- Item name (rice, beans, canned tuna, etc.)
- Quantity in storage
- Expiration date
- Recommended reserve (30–90 days)
- "Need to Buy" column highlights shortages automatically

3. Water & Energy Inventory

- Stored gallons & purification methods
- Fuel stock (firewood, propane, gasoline, solar battery levels)
- Generator hours logged
- Automatic reminders for replenishment

4. Medicine & First Aid Tracking

- Medicine name & dosage
- Expiration dates highlighted in red when near expiry
- Assigned family member (who needs it)

5. Tools & Equipment

- Flashlights, radios, generators, solar panels
- Condition (new, used, needs repair)
- Last maintenance date
- Spare parts availability

6. Family Go-Bag Checklist

- Cash, documents, emergency supplies, personal items
- ✅/❌ columns to quickly check readiness
- Weight tracker to ensure bags are portable

7. Barter & Skills Ledger

- List of items useful for trade (salt, batteries, soap, seeds)
- Family skills (carpentry, first aid, gardening)
- Notes on local trade partners

📌 How to Use It

1 Update Monthly – Set one day per month to check food, water, medicine, and supplies.

2 Color Alerts – Expiring items show in red, low reserves in yellow.

3 Budget Smarter – Track where your prepping money goes and adjust for efficiency.

4 Share with Family – Print or save as PDF for quick offline access.

⚡ Final Reminder:

Preparedness is not just stockpiling—it's **tracking and maintaining**. With this Excel Tracker, you'll always know what you have, what you need, and when to rotate supplies.

📌 **Downloadable Excel File:** Scan the QR code at the end of this book to get your **Budget & Inventory Tracker**.

ACKNOWLEDGMENTS

Dear Reader,

Thank you for spending your time—and your trust—on this book. My goal wasn't to predict the future, but to help you face it with clarity, courage, and a practical plan. If these pages helped you take even one step toward protecting your family, then they've done their job.

Preparedness is an act of love. Every gallon stored, every plan practiced, every neighbor you encourage makes your corner of the world steadier. You don't have to be perfect; you just have to begin—and keep going.

If this guide served you, please consider sharing it with someone who needs a nudge to get started. Your example may be the spark that builds a stronger family, a safer street, and a more resilient community.

You'll find all the printable tools and trackers via the QR code in the bonus section. Use them, adapt them, and make them your own. And when you've put this book to work, I'd be grateful if you left an honest review—your feedback helps more families find what they need.

Stand firm. Lead with calm. Build with hope.

With gratitude,

Mark Dortmiller

ABOUT THE AUTHOR

Mark Dortmiller is a preparedness writer and researcher dedicated to helping everyday families face uncertain times with confidence and clarity. With years of study in crisis response, financial resilience, and community survival strategies, Mark has developed a practical, family-first approach to preparedness.

Unlike doomsday scenarios that rely on fear, Mark's philosophy is rooted in responsibility, faith, and action. He believes that survival is not about isolation or stockpiling in secret—it's about building resilient households and stronger communities. His work blends historical lessons, modern strategy, and step-by-step checklists designed to be accessible for anyone, no matter their starting point.

When he isn't writing, Mark enjoys gardening, practicing self-reliance skills, and sharing preparedness knowledge with neighbors and local groups. His mission is simple: **empower families to become leaders in times of crisis, turning fear into readiness and uncertainty into strength.**